P9-BIE-166

Great business books distill a wide range of brilliant experiences and insights into light bulb moments and actionable steps for the reader. For leaders who want their businesses to thrive, being able to actualize differences as a competitive advantage is imperative. This book, from Jorge Luis Titinger, one of the most thoughtful CEOs I know, and his brilliant young entrepreneur co-author Pedro David Espinoza, is a nightstand essential for any leader who wants to build a business to thrive in the 21st century.

COCO BROWN | Founder & CEO of The Athena Alliance

It has long been recognized that inclusion and diversity are good for business, are good for the bottom line, and to empower a positive and rewarding culture for all. In this book Pedro David Espinoza and Jorge Luis Titinger have provided a compelling and actionable review of the issues, risks, opportunities and strategies to success-fully address them. They bring this to life with compelling insights and experiences from leaders who had successfully employed inclusion and diversity to innovate, empower and build leading organizations. A must read for the 21st century leader.

BILL COLEMAN | ex CEO of Veritas, CEO of BEA Systems, Board Member at Symantec, Operating Executive at The Carlyle Group

Differences That Make a Difference is a must read for anyone who wants invaluable examples from passionate leaders who realized that embracing diversity and inclusion can be a strategic advantage for successful organizations.

JOHN CLEVELAND | Chief Human Resources Officer at Seagate

Differences That Make A Difference by Pedro David Espinoza and Jorge Luis Titinger gives readers a spectrum of near rapid-fire opinions and thoughts about inclusion and diversity from an eclectic range of corporate and nonprofit leaders. Interesting food for thought.

JASON L. MA | Founder, CEO and Chief Mentor, ThreeEQ Inc., and Acclaimed Author of Young Leaders 3.0

Differences
That
Make a
Difference

Rocío,

Gracias por el apoyo.

Keep building the bridge.

PD.

Pedro David E.

We dedicate this book to the many individuals who have included us in teams, allowed us to make mistakes, shown us how not to, and put life into our work and work into our lives.

ABOUT THE FOREWORD & INTRODUCTION WRITERS

DR. PAT GELSINGER is the CEO of VMware, a global leader in cloud infrastructure and digital workplace technology with $8.97 billion in revenue in 2019. He is the author of *The Juggling Act*, a book on balancing work, family and faith in one's life, published originally in 2008 when he was the CTO at Intel, and since revised and expanded. In 2019 Pat was ranked best CEO in the US (he leads a worldwide team of 24,200 employees) by employment website Glassdoor, having received an astounding 99 percent approval rating.

DR. ANITA SANDS currently serves on the boards of directors at Symantec, Pure Storage, ServiceNow, ThoughtWorks, and AppBus, as well as on the advisory boards at DocuSign and Thrive Global. Originally from Ireland, Anita earned her both a Bachelor of Science in Applied Mathematics and a Ph.D. in Atomic & Molecular Physics at Queen's University Belfast, and a Masters in Public Policy and Management at Carnegie Mellon University. She is a sought-after speaker and advocate on issues such as board development and diversity and recently received the "Fearless Leader" Award from 2020 Women on Boards.

ABOUT THE AUTHORS

PEDRO DAVID ESPINOZA is *The Robin Hood of Technology* according to The Voice of America. He is an internet entrepreneur, angel investor, TEDx speaker, and author. At the age of 19, Pedro became the founder & CEO of SmileyGo, a platform that helps companies give smarter. In 2018, Pedro became the CEO of Alpaca Pan Peru (www.alpacapanperu.com), a social venture that empowers women to become entrepreneurs. At the age of 24, Pedro co-wrote a book with Jorge Titinger, with contributions from Eric Schmidt, Reed Hastings, and Pat Gelsinger among others.

Educated at Stanford and Berkeley, Pedro began his career as a car mechanic at Toyota. At the age of 17, Pedro composed and launched his music singles on Apple, Spotify, and Amazon. Pedro is an investor in companies such as Nadine West, Kiwi Campus, and Feed.FM. He's been a keynote speaker for the U.S. Patent and Trademark Office, the U.S. Chamber of Commerce, the World Intellectual Property Organization, and others.

Pedro has been profiled in Univision, Telemundo, Hispanic Shark Tank, and Forbes. In 2019, Pedro published a book *Differences That Make a Difference: How Organizations Succeed by Focusing on Innovation Through Inclusion* with Jorge Titinger (ex-CEO of SGI) by interviewing 175 global executives from Google, Netflix, Facebook, and many more.

He serves on the board of directors of Hertz Peru, Toyota Autoespar, and GESA.

JORGE LUIS TITINGER has built a multi-faceted career in the technology industry, having formed and led top-notch executive teams as well as executing two turnarounds as CEO [Verigy, Inc. and Silicon Graphics International (SGI)], with great results for all stakeholders. Today, Jorge runs Titinger Consulting, and provides strategy and leadership advice to several companies, focusing on the cultural dimension of executive teams and M&A integration. He is also a director with the Alliance of CEOs, a community of business leaders that focuses on deep strategic exchanges and the generation of new ideas for CEOs to bring to their businesses.

In addition to his work with Titinger Consulting, Jorge has served and continues to serve on the Boards of Directors of several public, private and non-profit organizations: CalAmp, Hispanic Foundation of Silicon Valley (including having served as chairman), Stanford Children's Hospital, Xcerra Corporation—now Cohu, AGP, and Innovate Public Schools. Indeed, he has been widely recognized for his work as well as his contributions to the community. He was the recipient of the Top 100 Latinos in Technology seven years in a row, and in 2017 received the Star Award from the Hispanic IT Executive Council. He was voted CEO of the year in 2013 by the CEO World Awards. In 2017, he was recognized by the Women's Leadership Council as one of the "Guys Who Get It" for his work in promoting women in Boards and on his executive teams.

Originally from Peru, Jorge received both his undergraduate and graduate degrees in Engineering and Management from Stanford University where he obtained. He was also an accomplished athlete, serving as captain of the Stanford varsity soccer team and later captain of the USA Indoor soccer national team. In addition, he has attained a third degree black belt in karate.

Differences That Make a Difference is Jorge's first book. He and his co-author, Pedro David Espinoza, leveraged their large networks and spoke with about 175 of the most recognized names in the industry. Using this vast source of insights, together with their own experiences, the two have succeeded in showing conclusively how inclusion and diversity have direct impact on the results and success of business.

PAN PERU
NONPROFIT ORGANIZATION

Given our backgrounds in entrepreneurship, business and technology, we believe that education is the best way to develop a community. Thus, we decided to support Pan Peru (www.panperu.org)—a nonprofit organization that builds libraries, computer labs, and greenhouses to empower the underserved youth of our Incan country.

We encourage you to support this charity as a fine way to educate economically disadvantaged children and women in Peru. Pan Peru has built nine libraries, six greenhouses, and four computer labs, benefiting 2,000 children in the most remote places of our Andean nation.

Equally important, Pan Peru launched Alpaca Pan Peru (www.alpacapanperu.com) with the mission to empower women to become entrepreneurs. This program is helping 28 women (single mothers, divorced, or teenagers) become businesswomen by training them on how to design, produce, and market their handmade alpaca garments, blankets, and sweaters.

You can support Pan Peru three ways:
PayPal: www.paypal.me/panperu
Venmo: @panperu
Web: www.panperu.org/web/donar-3/

Thank you,

Pedro and Jorge

AUTHORS' NOTE

The design of this book is intended to reflect its core message: the best products and services derive from a variety of perspectives and ideas. Our focus has been to bring together not only creditable research and reliable statistics, but the perspectives of individuals whose experiences inform how the business community has discovered the power of what those who operate in a competitive environment most often call "inclusion."

Frequently experts who write on this subject also include the word "diversity." We have purposefully chosen not to do that. Here is why. One does not introduce diversity to a group—when there are two or more people present, diversity is *there*.

"Diversity," like so many words, carries different meanings for different customers and colleagues and in different cases and contexts. Not to mention cultures. Native English speakers often quote the line from Gertrude Stein's poem: "A rose is a rose is a rose." And yet a rose to a botanist is quite different from what it is to a florist...or a bride-to-be...or a bee. (For what it's worth, a bee will ignore it if it's red!) And meaning is at the base of effective communication. So, ours is not an effort to dismiss or diminish the concepts that "diversity" present, but to move from that to what we consider to be the core issue: *inclusion*.

Here, too, we must pay close attention to meaning. If *inclusion* is taken to define the action through which a group that somehow considers itself superior is *allowing* access to another who either is not or has not yet proven himself or herself to be on the same level, isn't there yet another limiting assumption at work? If a group of youngsters playing a pick-up basketball game "allow" Kareem Abdul-Jabbar to join them, isn't that inclusion?

To harness the power of the concept, one must insist on its representing an environment within which each participant is presumed to have value, and will feel not only free to contribute but eager to do so. Consultant Verna Myers puts it best: "Diversity is being invited to the party. Inclusion is being asked to dance."[1]

And, we would add, be ready not only to waltz, but to shag, swing, hip-hop and maybe even end with a *plié*.

As you will see, our mode of inclusion in this book is to incorporate statistics, scientific studies, theories, opinions from the business community and relevant experiences of our own as well as those we know about.

Of course, we are eager for the interactive element to be added as well, and for that reason, please join us online at: www.pedroespinoza.com/blog.

Pedro David Espinoza and Jorge Luis Titinger, July 2019.

---

1   https://twitter.com/vernamyers/status/866451070779887616?lang=en.

FOREWORD By Dr. Pat Gelsinger

Research clearly demonstrates that diversity and inclusion in the workplace drive better business outcomes. Together, diversity and inclusion accelerate innovation, attract top talent, deepen employee engagement, and improve the bottom line. Capturing such benefits is impossible, however, unless we foster a culture that embraces everyone.

To begin, we must get clarity on how we define inclusion and the value it brings in a business context. Even as part of an industry working on some of the most complex technologies in the world, the tech industry hasn't yet cracked the code on D&I. This book provides a helpful roadmap for us to do exactly that.

Diversity is more than just diversity of gender or race—it's about diversity of thought, experience, perspective, skills and mindsets. More broadly, it extends to diversity in age, socio-economic background, and faith. When we take into account all of these nuanced differences, we put our organizations in a position to capture truly sustainable business advantages.

We cannot simply hire people with diverse backgrounds, skills, and mindsets, and expect magic to suddenly occur. We must go further by creating environments where people are empowered to show up and contribute as their true and authentic selves. That's where bold, breakthrough innovation happens.

If you look at who is making key decisions in business today, you'll see that it remains a very homogeneous group of leaders. We are not as diverse as we should be. That has to change. We all need to deepen our commitment to diversity and inclusivity. In my own organization, I recognize that begins with me.

Throughout my nearly 40 years working in tech, I've traveled my own path of discovery when it comes to diversity. I was just 18 years old when Intel first offered me a job interview on the West Coast. I very confidently informed my mother, " Don't worry, I'm not going there. They're crazy out in California. I'm a Pennsylvania farm boy!" At that point in my life I was the sheltered product of an extremely homogeneous community. Since then, I've had the opportunity to travel the world and work closely with people from every walk of life. I've had the good fortune to experience firsthand the incredible value that stems from diversity of thought and experience—both personally and professionally.

At VMware we've spent the last several years fostering what we call Power of Difference (POD) communities. It's been gratifying to see the positive impact of these employee-driven groups. They deepen and expand our company's inclusive culture by harnessing the power of human difference. I recall a particularly poignant moment not long ago when a member of our LGBQT POD revealed that s/he was initially afraid to reveal her/his sexual preference. Wow, that was a difficult moment. I realized that one of our employees simply did not feel safe sharing her/his authentic self at work. It was eye-opening because it's so critical that we provide a safe space for everyone. I recognized in that moment that I need to do better—and collectively our organization needs to do better. I've shared this story with leaders across our company and have asked them to commit to active listening and ongoing learning, so we can work together to foster a culture that is truly inclusive.

This is not a "we vs. they" construct; it's about all of "us" working to enact the environment in which we want to work. It is not the women or other underrepresented groups that need fixing; it's the companies and the environments that need to improve—cultivating talent and including everyone, regardless of gender, ethnicity, race, religion, age, sexual orientation, socio-economic status and other aspects of our identity that make us unique, whether one is a Californian technologist or Pennsylvanian farm boy. It is not for those perceived as different to force their way in or prove the validity of their perspective. It is for all of us to come together.

Together, we are our culture. Ultimately, it's not just the right thing to do, it's the smart thing to do.

In any organization, it's critical for people and teams to feel OK expressing divergent opinions. It's not always easy, but success lies in helping leaders become comfortable with the uncomfortable. This is something I'm consciously working on all the time. I've challenged myself to be more open and embracing of views and experiences that are radically different from my own. Core to this is an awareness of my own unconscious biases, because we all have them! Awareness lies at the heart of diversity and inclusion.

Bring your whole self to work, don't cultivate personas for different parts of your life. Equally important, encourage and expect your teams to do the same. Skills from one area of life are often surprisingly beneficial to another. These differences in thought, experience, background and culture form the foundation for high-performance teams that drive breakthrough innovation and better business outcomes.

ACKNOWLEDGMENTS

Producing a book is a process that refuses to stand aside and let other issues rule the day. And while it would be foolish to describe the days, weeks, months involved as a "life crisis," that time does present a certain kind of winnowing wherein the support of friends and colleagues takes new form not to mention special importance. And producing *this* book has been especially significant, because we found ourselves *living* the subject.

Our original idea has been transformed by the ideas and contributions of the people whose names appear throughout the book, as well as by the work of our production team. To ascribe to any one of that team only one kind of participation would be to denigrate her or his work, because each person time after time reached in to improve, to expand, to deepen the message. And included, really included on that team are people of various ages, genders, life experiences, and, of course, points of view.

So a Chicha Morada to the colleagues and family members who encouraged us, and to our team: Julia Ardiles, Hayley Bennett, Dr. Denise Duhon, Wendy Dunn, Pedro Espinoza (father), Dianna Espinoza, Dr. Karina Espinoza, Rachael Garrity, Vanessa Luna, Julia Smith, Staci Weber, and Daniel Yee.

ABOUT THIS BOOK

As we explained briefly in our authors' note, when one is engaged in the particular subject area we will together explore in the pages that follow, words and the meaning they carry can have a crucial impact. As part of our effort to be sensitive to that fact, we have adopted some procedures that might not make your fifth grade Language Arts teacher feel particularly comfortable, not to mention anyone trained in the rules of language usage for works published for the American English-speaking reader. To put it simply, we have more or less created our own style. It is, we argue, "inclusionary."

Here's how it's different:

1 – The superscript number directing you to the sources found in the End Notes for each chapter appear at the beginning of when the source is referenced, not at the end. Why? Because some of the referenced material is quite long, and we believe this is both clearer for you the reader and fairer to the individuals and organizations referenced.

2 – When a citation references a book, we do not include page numbers. If you refer to ebooks instead of hard copy volumes, page numbers are irrelevant. And, we anticipate translating this book into languages other than English for readers who, if they seek to find any of the sources, will most likely find them translated into another language, with different pagination. Idiosyncratic on our part? Probably. But in our own way, more inclusive.

In seeking individuals to interview for the Perspectives, we paid close attention to welcoming the full range of ideas and opinions. You will note, for example, that 80 are female and 80, male. Some interviews were conducted in Spanish—the native language for both of us—and the rest in English. We have been reasonably successful in spanning the generations, though the distribution is essentially a bell curve, leaning a bit to one side. Our own perspectives on that front provide a little mediation, since one of us is more than twice the age of the other.

Finally, here and now, front and center, we admit to a glaring exclusion. None of the individuals interviewed or the sources cited represents a "person-on-the-street" perspective. We have purposefully chosen 80 females and 80 males whose experiences have informed their business and social opinions about inclusion *as it affects the success of private enterprise and thereby innovative efforts for the common good.* While we have made every effort to be fair, transparent and accurate, this book was written by and for decision makers, present or future. The world is changing, and never have those decisions been more pivotal.

Our future is, indeed, ours to build.

INTRODUCTION By Dr. Anita Sands

Whoever once said that the "future ain't what is used to be" couldn't have been more prognostic. We live in one of the most exciting, transformative and disruptive times the world has ever seen, and while society and business have certainly undergone disruptive change in the past, what we haven't experienced is change of this magnitude, happening at this speed.

There are many factors that make today's environment unprecedented but for businesses in every sector, in every part of the world, the fact that two major tectonic plates are shifting beneath their feet leaves them particularly vulnerable this time around. Those plates are Digital Technologies and Demographics, and one is compounding and augmenting the effect of the other.

As the authors in this book correctly point out, almost 60 percent of the global population is Gen X-Y-Z in other words, aged 38 or under and if you subscribe to the notion that "demographics are destiny" then every business needs to pay attention to the inalienable impact of this fact. Layer on top the degree to which emerging technologies are redefining how we live, learn and work and it's obvious that every business needs to find a way to not only survive this transition but to thrive.

This calls for alternative strategies, different business models, changing operations, more effective innovation, and new ways of interacting with customers and employees alike. The key to navigating that successfully is a concept I refer to as "belonging," which in reference to the thoughtful study of "inclusion" brought forward by the authors can be seen as the ultimate outcome of successful diversity and inclusion efforts.

At the outset of their work, the authors explain their rationale for focusing on inclusion, accepting that diversity is almost a given in any circumstance where two or more people are present. I agree with their logic and have always seen diversity as a fact, whereas inclusion is an active choice. Put another way, you can think of diversity as the seeds, inclusion as the crop and belonging as the way in which you harvest both. The reason I believe so much in the power of belonging is because it is a feeling that every human being can relate to. Just like inclusion it is but the means to an end—the end being an innovative, successful future.

For businesses today, being innovative isn't a nice-to-have; it's a fundamental imperative. Diverse perspectives, new ideas, creativity, and risk-taking are the superpowers every company is trying to build. And yet, few have realized that their kryptonite is having employees who don't feel they are included or that they belong.

Closely linked to a culture of belonging is the notion of psychological safety—the belief that you're not at risk of embarrassment or rejection; that if you make a well-intentioned mistake, you won't be criticized.

In a culture where people feel included and psychologically safe, they'll feel confident enough to put an idea on the table and know that if it doesn't win out, it wasn't because of anything innately to do with them. This is what creates the trust that's needed for people to share their best thinking and put their craziest—and, perhaps, least popular—ideas on the table. And that is what lies at the heart of all innovation and transformation.

Not belonging renders people silent. After employers have worked so hard to recruit great employees, it's a shame to think that any of their talent or ingenuity remains untapped merely because they don't feel included and as a result, are hesitant to speak up. Worse still, when employees don't trust that they can express dissenting opinions without being punished, they'll only say what management wants to hear—killing any chance for innovation to occur.

Inclusion and belonging have the power to liberate ideas. Think of inclusion as the gateway through which your employees have to pass, and belonging as the key that ultimately unlocks it. Only when they've passed through that gate can they bring 100 percent of themselves to the job. Opening that gateway unleashes their creativity and tells them it's safe to take risks—the critical prerequisites for innovation and change.

Because the authors of this book have been quite intentional not only in researching issues, but in assuring that multiple viewpoints are shared, I believe they have not only presented but exhibited the value of inclusion. For many readers, it will not be possible to see just how true this is from merely reading names, backgrounds and ideas. But by my own rough count, I am relatively sure that the contributors here represent 30 countries, their ages range from the very early 20s to the late 70s, their values spill over from one political spectrum to another, and—this one's important—they feel absolutely comfortable presenting an idea with which they know others of their cohort will disagree. To put it simply, this book showcases what it sells.

Differences That Make a Difference

CHAPTER ONE

What You Name It Matters; How You Do It Matters More

The original outline for this book called for this chapter to deal with the definition of "diversity." The authors developed a list of decision-makers in various organizations to contact for their insights. It was, in part, this process that revealed that the definitions for the most part actually focused on inclusion as much as or more than they did diversity. Judy Little, Vice President of Strategic Alliance Management at Ericsson until two years ago, points out that the ideas that spell growth come from "diversity of thought from people with different backgrounds and experiences." She adds that recruiting is just the beginning, and that providing ways for individuals to move up within the organization is equally important.

Not surprisingly, Ericsson as an organization sees inclusion not as an objective, but as a crucial means of achieving their objective, which is to "attract, develop, engage, advance and retain a high-performing workforce."

Clearly, in organizations like Ericsson, that high-performing workforce is one that has been chosen to:

- reflect the anticipated customer base;
- have the skills to articulate not only near-term tactical goals, but longer term strategic plans;
- and be ready to enrich the innovative side of the corporate environment.

Perhaps the most revealing investigation has to do with exactly how many perspectives must be included to create the most successful mix. Or, put another way: What divides people enough that their perspectives differ? Certainly gender, race, sexual orientation, country of origin, and age are standard. But disabilities often matter, too, as do religious/ethical values and life experience that includes travel or living in less than homogenous communities. And the combination of any two or three of these can and does create an entire array of subsets.

Consider, for example, this scenario. Your employer is in pharmaceuticals, and is considering the acquisition of a company supposedly well along in research and development having to do with cloning. Your plan is to make the decision by the close of the fiscal year, which is eight months away. At the meeting next week, you will be voting on who is to fill the two openings on the board of directors, which to date includes four white males, all physicians—one in his 60s, one in his 50s, and two just out of medical school; an Hispanic, female pharmacist; a German engineer, who also is Jewish and the father of a rabbi; a Japanese astrophysicist, who is confined to a wheelchair and roundly kidded about being this generation's Stephen Hawking; the CEO (who is gay) and the CFO—that's you! The search has narrowed the candidates for the two positions to four people:

Rosanna Esperanzo is a hospice nurse who has a master's degree in physics, and uses her science background to tutor middle schoolers whose first language is Spanish.

Nigel Rimmel has just moved to the US from Switzerland. He is 74, has founded and sold two aerospace companies, continues to serve on a couple of boards of privately held companies in Belgium, and is not all that happy that his wife's very precarious health situation has necessitated the move to this country.

Jorge Contrera has just sold a very lucrative video game business, lucrative because it holds the patent to a game he developed in the 1990s. His hobby is hang-gliding, he tends to prefer lavender dress shirts and Chinos, and is definitely not, as he stresses, "a morning person."

Meredith Mosely, who is 37 (we think, but she could be older), lives on a Texas ranch she inherited from her father. If she is chosen for the board, she will be the only member who has actually owned a drone. And the only psychologist.

Whom would you choose and why? If you like such exercises, write your answers down. If not, just remember them.

Clearly, yours is a company that has already demonstrated its appreciation for the value of inclusion. But on what premises?

When you have made your choices, and at least taken a stab at what you believe those premises to be, read on. You will find below the four candidates' descriptions changed, each by only a word or a phrase.

Rosanna Esperanzo is a nun and a hospice nurse who has a master's degree in physics, and uses her science background to tutor middle-schoolers whose first language is Spanish.

Nigel Rimmel has just moved to the US from Switzerland. He is 74, has founded and sold two aerospace companies, continues to serve on a couple of boards of privately held companies in Belgium, and is not all that happy that his divorce from his third wife has necessitated the move to this country.

Jorge Contrera has just sold a very lucrative video game business, lucrative because it holds the patent to a game he developed in the 1990s. His hobby is hang-gliding, he tends to prefer jeans and beat-up high-top sneakers, and is definitely not, as he stresses, "a morning person."

Meredith Mosely, who is 37 (we think, but she could be older), lives on an Australian ranch she inherited from her father. If she is chosen for the board, she will be the only member who has actually owned a drone. And the only psychologist.

Now whom do you choose? Any changes? Did you notice—or did it matter to you—that there were no Asians or African Americans, at least none so described? Not a lot of demonstrated skill on the financial side of operations? How about legal considerations? With what life experience are prospective buyers of the clones likely to identify?

The point here is to demonstrate that each of us, based on her or his own background and experience, imputes characteristics to people from not merely one or two pieces of information, but from the "cluster" and what kind of portrait we believe it paints.

I am Mexican, but I look white. I'm automatically judged by my name, yet I'm treated differently when someone looks at me."

~ Rodrigo Garza | CEO Flexinvest

The tension between providing a safe environment so that board members, corporate leaders and employees feel free to express themselves and at the same time adhering to the core values of an inclusive organization is all too real, and our launch pad for the chapters that follow.

In the section below, you will see a collection of research that solidly supports the importance of inclusion in creating and sustaining successful enterprises. With that as a given, how then do wise leaders optimize the inclusion advantage?

STATISTICALLY SPEAKING

The original McKinsey 2015 report[1] indicated that companies in the top quartile for inclusion on their executive teams were 15 percent more likely to experience above-average profitability than companies in the fourth quartile. The 2018 report[2] found an increase to 21 percent. Nonetheless, women and minorities remain under-represented. Looking globally, Australian companies take the lead when comparing the women's share of executive roles— 21 percent vs 19 percent in the US and 15 percent in the United Kingdom. The McKinsey hypothesis continues to be that more diverse companies are able to attract top talent and to improve their customer orientation, employee satisfaction and decision-making.

As part of its "What If I Told You" series[3], Goldman Sachs Research defines Gen-Z as those born in 1998 and after. There are 70+ million, they don't remember a world without the Internet and their ability to navigate online has made them eager to bargain. Much thriftier than Millenials, they also are heavily entrepreneurial. A recent *Harvard Business Review* article reports that seven in ten teens are "self-employed' (selling goods on eBay, teaching music lessons, etc.) As a burgeoning group of potential customers and employees, their sheer numbers call for a new kind of inclusion.

In June 2017, 175 companies signed on to the "CEO Action for Diversity and Inclusion" designed to ensure that:

...inclusion is core to our workplace culture and that our businesses are representative of the communities we serve. Moreover, we know that diversity is good for the economy; it improves corporate performance, drives growth and enhances employee engagement.

~ *Forbes* Magazine June 12, 2017

PERSPECTIVES ON POINT

Insights Gained from Personal Interviews by the Authors

JESSICA STRAUSS, a Kauffman Fellow, was serving as Vice President at the National Venture Capital Association when our interview took place. That experience, plus her involvement in a number of other professional and community activities, meant she had a firsthand look at how inclusion plays out in a variety of settings. She makes the point that in addition to the kinds of differences one can physically catalog—age, gender, ethnicity, etc.—there is what she refers to as "diversity of experience." Shared life experiences between employees and customers or potential customers she argues provide a means of better understanding the customer base and can even smooth the way for a company wishing to break through into a new demographic. An inclusive workforce, as she puts it, can have a "cascade effect."

ATUL SINGH is Founder and CEO of FairObserver, a not-for-profit media organization based in the US, with partners—some multinational (such as The World Bank), some academic, some analytical, some focused on national and global policy, the full gamut—throughout the globe. It boasts a network of more than 2,000 contributors. Singh notes that the "news business" is largely populated by the "white, male, Ivy-League-educated," few of whom have ever been impoverished or struggled in other ways. As an immigrant, he, himself, has felt excluded because of his ethnicity and the fact that his "roots" were in underserved communities, but he also has found that this affords a competitive advantage.

JENNA NICHOLAS is focused—on what works, what matters, who cares, who commits, and why the time is now. She has wrapped her zeal for making a difference in educational achievements at Oxford and Stanford Universities (including an MBA at the latter) and is motivated by the idea that talent is evenly distributed but opportunity is not. Currently, she is CEO of Impact Experience, an enterprise that creates collaborations among innovators, investors, philanthropists, entrepreneurs and leaders of marginalized communities. Underestimated communities are the focus, and the initiatives include activating investors to support activities such as addressing health disparities, retraining workers whose jobs have been subsumed by technology, and unlocking capital for women and people of color who run businesses and funds. In our interview, when we asked how she thinks about inclusion, she shared an image from her Baha'i Faith, which depicts "men and women being like two wings of a bird, where both are necessary for the bird to fly.... It is necessary to have a broad range of perspectives and backgrounds represented so that flight can occur."

LINDRED GREER analyzes, speaks about, consults on, teaches about—generally is an expert on—the structure and behavior of teams, what works and what doesn't, what kind of leaders create winning teams, hierarchies hither and yon. As a member of the faculty at the Stanford Graduate School of Business, she essentially represents the "ground zero" perspective when it comes to identifying how organizations can both exert control over and be controlled by inclusion. In academia, she says, "any difference that makes a difference" fits within the inclusion spectrum. She also argues the campus scene is improving, and it is now up to companies to make better use of the pipeline, so that hiring, training and promoting all happen equitably—and therefore, with better profitability.

ESTUARDO RODRIGUEZ has quite literally spent his life in and around the political arena. Having grown up in DC, he has worked in political campaigns, as an attorney for the US Department of Housing and Urban Development, as an analyst for the US State Department, as a lobbyist, and as an advisor on state, regional and national levels. As Founder and Principal of the Raben Group, he specializes in advising clients in the financial and telecommunications industries, as well as various not-for-profit organizations. On the subject of inclusion, he is forthright: "First, remember altruism makes financial sense. You can and should make sure your business grows, and know at the same time there is nothing wrong with doing the right thing. Yes, you CAN make money doing it. A solid value system builds brand loyalty." Or as the Raben Group mission statement phrases it: "We were founded with a lofty goal and an audacious spirit: to make this nation greater and to move public policy in a sensible, humane direction."

CLAUDIA ROMO EDELMAN has played a number of distinguished roles in the global arena, working with organizations such as the World Economic Forum, the United Nations High Commission for Refugees, and UNICEF, to mention only three. She currently is Special Advisor to the We Are All Human Foundation, an organization she founded. A paragraph from the vision statement on the foundation's website briefly explains Edelman's perspective on world affairs:

> We Are All Human Foundation is dedicated to bursting bubbles and revealing a world of abundance where everyone has enough air to breathe. Inclusion is not just a moral imperative, it is the smart choice. Openness enhances a

person's beauty, inside and out. With a broader perspective, we shift from fearing limitations to appreciating the beauty in the world and inside of us.[4]

In our interview, Edelman is particularly firm in her insistence that the focus should be not on what exists, but what is recognized. As she puts it: "What is needed is the discussion. We are already diverse. What is needed is not to create it, but accept it."

SHANNON GORDON has made it to a career juncture that lots of people would say is nearly impossible: as CEO of theBoardlist (where gender diversity on boards of directors is the primary focus), she is both doing and being what she believes in. And though we didn't ask her precisely, we're pretty sure she would agree that her career path was a pretty direct route. For example, it included a Peace Corps stint in Senegal, which she remembers taught her firsthand what it is like to not be part of any majority, so that "in every way you speak from a different perspective." Then there was the rigorous research and goal-driven teamwork as an engagement manager for McKinsey & Company, customer focus at Walmart. com and Shyp...and more. "Actually," she says, "it was in business school that I first learned that inclusion drives performance. For me, inclusion is defined pretty simply: incorporating different perspectives in ideation, innovation and decision-making."

KELLIE MCELHANEY, serves as a Distinguished Teaching Fellow at the University of California, Berkeley, where she is also Founding Director of the Center for Gender, Equity and Leadership at the Haas School of Business. She has little patience for those who insist they "don't wish to be a token." She agrees instead with Rosalind Brewer, COO of Starbucks, who says: "Yes, we're hiring you because you're different. Be proud of it!" And when it comes to inclusion, McElhaney has a brisk, telling description: "Diversity is counting heads. Inclusion is making heads count." In *Just Good Business*, her book on corporate social responsibility, McElhaney points out that while often the term "social responsibility" is interpreted to mean attention to community, global and conservation issues, such as environmentalism and social welfare, it applies equally to harnessing the power of fairness and inclusion within the corporate structure.

GABY NATALE is, for those who are fluent in Spanish, a *nombre conocidísimo*. She has won three Daytime EMMY awards as host and executive producer of "SuperLatina." She not only owns the rights to her television show, but also a television studio; and she has worked in a number of other reporting and news analysis roles. She is crisp and to the point when she defines inclusion. "Fitting in," she says, "means that one adapts: one fits the mold of another. Belonging means one is accepted as is.... I believe that inclusion should be seen as the space of belonging. Create a space of belonging and accept people as they are 100 percent."

MO FATHELBAB, Founder and CEO of Forum Resources Network (See Chapter 7 Perspectives for a description of his company.) moved to the US from Egypt when he was a child and has a vivid memory of what it means to feel included—or not. As chance would have it, during his first week in public elementary school in the US, he was seated between a white girl on one side, and a black girl on the other. The white girl asked him if he were "black." Puzzled, he really didn't know how to answer, but he chose "No." The black girl said: "Didn't you say you moved from Egypt and isn't that in Africa?" When he nodded, she closed the subject: "Then you're black." That evening, when he related the exchange to his mother, she suggested that the next time he explain that in his home country people were not divided into racial categories. Now a father himself, Fathelbab says he teaches his son to "see everyone as in the same group, and then search for the differences that make them special."

DIANA LUTFI came to the United States as a toddler with her mother, who was fleeing an intractable family situation in Indonesia. Her mother was detained and held for six weeks, so Diana has close, personal experience with some of the difficulties facing immigrants. A 2017 graduate of the University of California, Berkeley, she established at the university a credit-bearing course entitled "Faith and Reasons," to both give students an opportunity to discuss controversial topics and receive appropriate counseling as needed. A TEDx speaker, she focuses on topics such as access for the disadvantaged. In her opinion, in the corporate world as well as the nation at large, it is far easier to solve almost any problem if one is able to adapt to the values of another individual or group. Speaking the language, she asserts, is not enough. It is crucial to "speak the culture."

LAURA GOMEZ is CEO of Atipica, a company formed specifically to develop "the world's first inclusive AI for the talent lifecycle." As a child she moved to the US from Mexico, and was separated from her family. She insists, though, that because she eventually was documented, her challenges have been quite different from those known as "DACA" immigrants today. Through her personal experience, as well as through the multiple organizations with which she has become affiliated—Project Include, Diversity Council, Women of Color Council of the Anita Borg Institute for Women and Technology, Silicon Valley Council—she believes that, as she puts it, "We have to have difficult conversations to have progress." She explains that those conversations must address the issues of access and privilege. "This is not an Olympics of oppression," she insists. "The point isn't who is more oppressed than whom. Instead, it is the need to acknowledge what systems provide access more to some than to others. It's time to call out the individuals who fail to admit that there are those who cannot afford to fail, for whom being good is not enough. They are required to be the best to be allowed in." Or, as she wrote in a LinkedIn post: "Inclusion does not happen by accident. It is intentional, thoughtful work."

CRISTINA LONDONO has spent more than two decades with Telemundo, the Spanish language television network owned by NBCUniversal, based in both the San Francisco and Washington, DC, offices. In addition to her general reporting assignments, she has in the last few years taken a special interest in increasing awareness of and organizing support for immigrant workers, especially those employed in agriculture, who suffer debilitating health conditions. Her perspective on inclusion in the US is crisp and to the point: "The problem with inclusion and diversity is that the United States is a country that is changing at a giant pace. So I think that now the population is Asian, the population is Hindu, that the growth of inclusion has to include more people and more diversity, and be more distinct, and brings customs that are not necessarily ours."

ANITA SANDS serves on the boards of directors of ServiceNow, Symantec, Pure Storage and Thoughtworks, as well as on the advisory boards of Thrive Global and Docusign. In many ways, she represents the idea of what she likes to call "belonging" (on the premise that inclusion has come to be defined as a zero-sum game by those insiders who fear it will somehow dilute their own power and authority) as strongly as she promotes it. Holding a Master's Degree in Public Policy and Management from Carnegie Mellon and a PhD in Atomic and Molecular Physics from Queen's University Belfast, she brings experience and thought processes that reach well beyond the norm in the business world. If she were asked to respond to our exercise regarding the board of the pharmaceutical acquisition, she would most probably point out that the board as it is presently constructed is already ahead of the game because: (1) it includes members below the age of 50; (2) it includes women; (3) it is multi-cultural; and (4) the choices appear to have been made more on life and operational experience than on prior board experience. "I don't agree with people who insist that there are not enough qualified candidates for board appointments, that it's a supply-side problem," she says. "It's on the demand side in most cases, and there are three basic flaws. 'Qualified' means: 1. Being a current or former CEO or CFO; 2. Having prior board experience; 3. Being known to someone on the board." Boards, Sands adds, are for "foresight, oversight, and insight," and she stresses that whatever you call it—diversity, inclusion, or belonging—it is "the solution not the problem."

COREY ANTHONY has spent close to a quarter of a century working at AT&T, an experience that he enthusiastically describes as "multiple careers, but I never had to leave AT&T." Much of that time found him in operational roles—finance, marketing, sales, cybersecurity, etc.—but when the individual whose responsibility included supporting inclusion issues decided to retire, he was quick to apply for the position. He is equally quick to point out that as Senior Vice President, Human Resources, and Chief Diversity Officer, he is not an enforcer. He explains:

> No, I am in no way the police, I'm a partner, a champion. I spend zero calories at all trying to convince anyone in a leadership role of the value of inclusion. AT&T is way beyond that stage. Yes, we're a data-driven company, so we do look at statistics, but certainly not as a way of penalizing. For us, it's a way of gauging the process, and at the same time making sure that nothing we do has unintended consequences.

Must be a pretty successful way of operating. In 2019, DiversityInc named AT&T number one among the 50 top companies for inclusion and diversity.

RON ESTRADA, you might say, has been on a roll, except "rolls" normally last a week if you're lucky and Estrada is into years now. In the last four, he has chalked up both the Austin, Texas, Businessman of the Year and the Univision President and CEO Employee Special Recognition Rewards. Plus he was named one of the Top 100 Diversity Executive Leaders by *Diversity MBA* magazine, as well as one of the 2018 Top 100 Corporate Responsibility Influence Leaders by Assent Compliance. In addition to his "day job" as Corporate Responsibility & Community Empowerment Executive for Univision, he serves as Vice Chair of the Congressional Hispanic Caucus Institute. In a phrase, he "knows more than a little bit about inclusion." And what he knows drives what he projects, which is near the top of the "This Is Happening" scale. On the business front, he insists "We are way beyond the time when inclusion was a 'human resources issue.' It's part of basic operation strategy. Lots of statistics and actual corporate experiences have proven its importance." And in the larger community, he sees affinity groups, especially the Latina/Latino ones with which he works, becoming collaborative, cohesive and active. "This is becoming a united community that is no longer 'waiting for the moment' to step up," he insists.

ENDNOTES

[1] Vivian Hunt, Dennis Layton and Sara Prince, "Diversity Matters," (McKinsey and Co., 2015), https://assets.mckinsey.com/~/media/ 857F440109AA4D13A54D9C496D86ED58.ashx.

[2] Vivian Hunt, Sara Prince, Sundiatu Dixon-Fyle, and Lareina Yee, "Delivering through Diversity," (McKinsey and Co., 2018), https://www.mckinsey.com/~/ media/mckinsey/business%20 functions/organization/our%20insights/delivering%20through%20diversity/delivering-through-diversity_full-report.ashx.

[3] Robert D. Boroujerdi and Christopher Wolf, CFA, "What If I Told You," (Goldman Sachs Research, 2015), https://www.goldmansachs.com/insights/pages/macroeconomic-insights-folder/what-if-i-told-you/report.pdf.

[4] https://www.weareallhuman.org/who-we-are/.

CHAPTER TWO

Clues to Inclusion

—

Typically, discussions of inclusion in the workplace focus on social and cultural norms and how they affect the perceptions, definitions, and behaviors that surround the issue. While there are certainly valuable insights that arise from those discussions, the focus of this book is a bit different. There are three seminal questions:

1. What effect does the practice of inclusion have on the ability of the business to grow?
2. Is it possible to demonstrate how it affects the bottom line?
3. What about success at innovation?

Social scientists—economists and behaviorists alike—often talk in terms of quantitative and qualitative data. Some insist that the research-driven statistics that constitute the quantitative investigation are more reliable, because they are more objective. Others argue that the extrapolations from those numbers as well as the introduction of information gleaned from interviews and behavioral studies are a necessary component of any comprehensive investigation.

For our purposes, let's say both are descriptive and predictive.

THE NUMBERS, PLEASE

It would take a much larger book than this one is designed to be to include all of the research on the issue of inclusion that has been carried out in North America in the last decade, not to mention in other countries. Certainly one of the most-often cited is the 2015 investigation by McKinsey & Co entitled "Diversity Matters"[1] that we mentioned in Chapter One. Diversity in this case is defined as leadership (top management and boards of directors) that includes more females and is more mixed on the racial/ethnic spectrum. Constituting the study group are more than 340 large, public companies operating in Canada, Latin America, and the United Kingdom, as well as in the United States.

The researchers divided the group into quartiles and discovered that those in the top quartile in terms of gender diversity were 15 percent more likely to have financial returns above their national industry median. The same comparison on the basis of ethnic diversity revealed more than double that amount: 35 percent to be exact. Of course, those reporting these results caution that this does not prove that diversity *causes* the better performance, but instead that "companies that commit to diverse leadership are more successful."

Three years later, in a follow-up study, "Delivering through Diversity,"[2] also referenced briefly in Chapter One, McKinsey broadened its scope to include 1,000 companies in 12 countries and used two measures of financial performance: profitability (based on the average earnings before taxes margin) and what they term "value creation" or the economic profit margin. Finally, the researchers looked beyond leadership levels to include the work force in their analysis.

The trends identified earlier persist, and the researchers suggest that reasons could derive from:

Talent—better access

Decision-making—informed and enhanced

Consumer insight—deepened and strengthened

Employees—more engaged and reacting to a "license to operate."

$$$

In another 2018 report,[3] Richard Warr, professor of finance at NC State University, and his coauthors Roger Mayer and Jing Zhao, argue that a study of the 3,000 largest publicly traded companies in the US does indeed prove a causative link—not merely correlation—between strong inclusion practices and better performance at developing innovative products and services. The measure? Patent and patent-citation data, and new product announcement data between 2001 and 2014.

$$$

A collaborative study[4] by the Boston Consulting Group and the Technical University of Munich provides ample corroboration. This one involves German, Swiss and Austrian companies. Researchers found that as the proportion of women in management increases, so, too, does innovation, defined in this instance by the percentage of revenue from new products and services in the most recent three-year period. How much? With a female proportion of 10 percent and below, the median level of innovation revenue stalls at 15 percent. At double the female complement, it jumps to 25 percent.

$$$

A 2016 Gallup.com study[5] published in the *Journal of Leadership and Organizational Studies* found that companies with higher than average gender diversity and employee engagement displayed

46 to 58 percent better financial performance than those falling below the median.

$$$

In a November 2018 article in *Barrons*,[6] Cindy Chen Delano, a senior legal analyst for distressed investments at Whitebox Advisors, reports the HFRX Diversity Women index, reflecting returns linked to women-run hedge funds, had outperformed the HFRI Fund Weighted Composite over the previous three, five and 10 years.

$$$

Focusing specifically on the tech sector of the US economy, Intel and Dalberg Global Development Advisors published a report[7] in 2016 that suggested improvement in inclusion of women and multiple ethnic groups had the potential to create as much as $570 billion in value and in turn add between 1.2 and 1.6 percent to the national GDP. The findings derive from a study of more than 170 tech companies and include a full series of data points, which the authors describe as evidence of correlation, not causation, as they call for additional research.

> My favorite quote on this subject [attributed to Canadian Prime Minister Justin Trudeau] is: Diversity is a fact; inclusion is a choice.
>
> ~ Dan Schulman | CEO of Paypal

WORDS TO
THE WISE

It is interesting to note that:

1 – In more recent times, McKinsey and other researchers have reversed the order of the acronym, referring now to *I and D* rather than *D and I*. Further to the importance of inclusion.

2 – Having productive discussions on the subject, not to mention formulating efficient action plans, can founder when there is insufficient agreement on exactly what constitutes I and D. Those who dismiss it as "PC," by which they may mean "pretty controversial" as well as "politically correct," most normally stick with the core list of gender, gender preference, age, race and ethnicity. Others add to that the disabled, and the disenfranchised. Still others incorporate representatives of different points of view, such as entrepreneurial vs bureaucratic; rural vs metropolitan; liberal vs conservative; family-owned vs publicly traded; European vs American. And finally there are those who deal in various personality or performance indices—the DISC, Myers-Briggs, the Enneagram, etc.

In a series of interviews, we asked for a definition of "diversity," and the variance of responses listed on the Perspectives on Point pages in this book illustrates that answers and attitudes are, well, *diverse*.

3 – It is important to consider that the very existence of an inclusive environment can have effects that have little to do with who is including whom. The change agent may be the simple fact that inclusion is occurring.

Social psychologist Henri Tajfel[8] discovered a phenomenon most commonly referred to as "minimal group identification" that sheds new light on human tendencies to identify with as well as reject others with no real foundation to do so. In his experiment, he ushered a group of subjects into his lab where he had positioned a screen on which he flashed a series of dots. After he asked them to estimate how many there were, he put them into categories: underestimators vs overestimators; accurate vs inaccurate. Once he had collected them into groups based on those categories, he asked them to divide money among the members of all the groups. What he found was that his subjects showed a measurable preference for—and thereby gave more money than was proportionate to—the members of their own group.

4 – The numbers reported above deal for the most part with inclusion within organizational leadership. There is, perhaps, not as much research about its effects throughout the organization, and on customer service as well as product development, but those effects do exist.

In an April 2018 post for *Forbes*,[9] Paolo Gaudiano, Founder of Aleria (a firm devoted to helping not just corporate America, but human society become more inclusive and equitable), argues that inclusion should not be a company's goal, or a condition you impose, but instead an outcome of your efforts to maximize the company's performance. As he explains: "In other words, you should focus on achieving inclusion, and track diversity as a measure of your success."

He goes on to create what he calls a "thought experiment," in which two employees are hired for the same job. They are the same age, attended the same school, essentially are identical except that one is male and the other female. If the majority of the existing employees are male, whether the two have equally comfortable experiences derives overwhelmingly from how those employees treat the female. The less inclusive they are, the less likely she is to succeed—or to stay.

From her experience at Harvard Business School, where her classes included students from various countries, Kaia Simmons (See Chapter 9 Perspectives for more information.) points out that there is a stark difference between intellectually knowing something is true and feeling it. In discussions of complex issues, she says, being able to feel another person's experience broadens one's world view. Be it a classroom or a workplace, if you don't feel comfortable talking, you remain siloed. She concludes that inclusion happens in an open culture where people are not afraid to speak and those who are speaking are not too easily offended.

PERSPECTIVES ON POINT

Insights Gained from Personal Interviews by the Authors

ALLAN BURNS, CEO of Paradise Petroleum Marketers, LLC, has lots of everyday experience with issues of inclusion because of the cultural diversity of South Florida, where he lives and works. Asked how he would suggest convincing other owners and operators of small and medium-sized businesses that it is a good thing to include employees from different cultures in the workforce, he answers right away. "I've seen it as almost a trade secret," he says, explaining that for him having access to different ethnic communities is advantageous in multiple ways. An employee from a specific group creates an entrée to better marketing to that group, a phenomenon that he found was quite helpful when he hired a Cuban American for a management position. So, simply put, an inclusive workforce automatically increases the company's reach. And, he adds, in his experience many individuals who identify strongly with the values shared by their ethnic group(s) are intensely loyal if they believe they are being treated fairly. The stability his company derives from that loyalty gives him a measurable advantage when competing with larger firms where the corporate climate is not the same.

ALEX NOWRASTEH speaks from a quite different point of view. As Senior Immigration Policy Analyst at the Center for Global Liberty and Prosperity, a part of the Cato Institute, Nowrasteh writes for the US print media (*Wall Street Journal, Washington Post,* etc.), is co-author of a booklet "Open Immigration, Yea and Nay," and also has contributed to a number of academic publications. His expertise on immigration issues is in demand, too, for commentary on the full range of television networks dealing with public policy issues—Fox News, MSNBC, Bloomberg, NPR, plus regional and local stations and channels. While it may be on a more macroeconomic scale, he agrees wholeheartedly with Allan Burns that the multicultural nature of the US is one of its greatest assets. "It is no accident," he insists, "that this is the strongest economy in the world. In many ways, we are strengthened by a cyclical pattern. Immigrants—not just random immigrants, but those who are the more ambitious, the risk-takers—*choose* to come here. When they are included, their enthusiasm and loyalty feed the economic growth, which in turn makes the country more attractive to others like them."

Nowrasteh describes the current US economy as not only the most diverse in the world, but the most diverse in history.

> Dealing with what we have now actually requires input from different backgrounds, a collaboration among those with different ideas and from different backgrounds. That's not new. It is part of what America is. If you look at the ancestries of today's US population, it is evident we are like no other country in the world.

Asked to describe how he would define inclusion, Nowrasteh stresses the importance of ideas. "If I were to be forced to make a choice between a group that looks and dresses differently, maybe speaks differently, and one that represents a wide range of backgrounds, ideologies and ideas, it is the latter I would choose every time."

BEN MUNOZ (not the actor—we should have asked him if he gets fan mail!) is the Co-founder and CEO of Nadine West, an online women's fashion subscription service that's the leader in this industry niche. He says that for his company inclusion is "organic." Because the goods are priced lower than those of most all competitors, the Nadine West customer base itself includes women from a wide arrange of socioeconomic positions.

> For us, it's just practical, good business sense, because we employ people who are part of the same demographic range that describes our customers. Generally speaking, about half our employees are non-white, and probably a quarter don't speak English. And those of us who see the demographic shift that is imminent are pretty sure that if companies wish to survive they will need to provide offerings and price them in ways that will attract the full customer base.

And, by the way, Munoz is also Founder and CEO of BensFriends.org, a network of support communities for individuals with one or another rare disease. His own experience with one such disease taught him the value of peer support even outside the corporate arena.

JAN D'ALESSANDRO has leadership experience in the Tech world that includes the likes of AOL, Yahoo, Topspin Media, etc. As Co-founder and President of Blue J Strategies, and legal advisor and consultant to multiple firms, she has worked with a wide variety of organizational cultures and management teams. "What is interesting," she notes, "is that training in such areas as sexual harassment is mandated based on the number of employees and varies by state." The training also varies by level of employment, with some states specifying supervisors and/or managers, and others all employees.

MARCO GIBERTI is Founder and CEO of Vesuvio Ventures, based in the Miami/Ft. Lauderdale area of Florida, the most recent expression of his infectious enthusiasm about the potential success to be derived from the support of entrepreneurship. He is bullish about the future of the US economy, and in our interview sums up two strong beliefs on which he bases that opinion. "I believe this country will grow in intelligence as it continues to receive and include minorities and immigrants and the productivity they bring," he explains, "and I also believe that any program involving entrepreneurship education generates employment, wealth, and a social solution."

PAT GELSINGER is keenly aware of how important it is for C-suite executives to not only understand, but actively manage the data around which their digital businesses are built. As CEO of VMware, he deals with the full spectrum of technological innovation, and knows why strong leadership is key. Inclusion happens, he says, when leaders pay attention at all levels. "As an example, we have at least one female on every hiring team, and insist that every candidate group be a mix, too. What's more, our executives know that part of their pay is determined by how well they do on the subject." It's clear that his is not merely a theoretical or ideological approach, but a practical one, built into all kinds of decision-making. As he sums it up: "It takes top down diligence and bottom-up programs." With a reported 500,000 enterprise customers now on their list, clearly VMware knows something about good business practices.

LILI GIL VALLETTA turned being what could have been considered a "victim" of faulty inclusion practices into being an "expert" on not just inclusion, but cultural intelligence. She was 17 when she arrived in the US from Colombia, with no English skills. Now a business leader and Co-founder and a tech innovator, she serves or has served on multiple boards—Harvard Women's Leadership, National YMCA—and advisory groups— NYC Technology Leadership Advisory Council, New York State Council on Women and Girls—and frequently is a commentator on national television. She describes the mission of her company, Culturintel, as using artificial intelligence to provide clients with insights that will inform and improve decision-making, by representing "the real-time and unsolicited voice of the people." (From her LinkedIn page.) How does she do it? She told us: "I want to make sure I am surrounded by people who are smarter than I am, and that includes the people on my team, as well as the people who guide me, advise me, champion me."

TODD SCHULTE is the President of FWD.us, a lobbying organization that focuses on immigration, criminal justice and education. Among the founders of the organization are Bill Gates and Mark Zuckerberg, so his is a job operated "on stage" a good amount of the time. Schulte works closely with immigration issues himself, and notes that until very recently the United States has been perceived internationally as a "magnet for talent," not only because of the strength of the economy, but also because of its first-rate universities, and a populace that is welcoming. He agrees that the US immigration system is not perfect, and that monitoring and improving security is crucial, but stresses that by making immigration the focus of political discourse and unrest decision-makers and the public at large might lose sight of the fact that modern history proves that immigration as we have heretofore experienced it improves the lives of all Americans and, again incorporated effectively, the stability and growth of America's businesses, large and small.

CHRISTOPHER REYNOLDS has a life story that sounds as if it could have been written by a Hollywood screenwriter. The son of an auto plant worker and a registered nurse, he grew up in Detroit. After graduating from college, with a Phi Beta Kappa key tucked snugly in his possession, he went to Harvard Law School, clerked for a Circuit Court judge in Detroit, and served as an Assistant United States Attorney in the criminal division of the U.S. Attorney's Office, Southern District of New York. Then, before joining Toyota in 2007, he was a partner in a New York law firm. Today he is Chief Administrative Officer, Manufacturing & Corporate Resources for Toyota North America, as well as Deputy Chief Officer, General Administration & Human Resources Group for Toyota Motor Corporation.

Having written all that, it seems a bit redundant to describe Reynolds as "articulate," but that he is, especially in delineating not only the values that define Toyota corporate policy when it comes to inclusion, but also explaining why research makes it clear that inclusion bolsters sales as well as branding. Here's just part of what he has to say on those two points:

> For us, Diversity & Inclusion is all about creating a culture where everyone can thrive, regardless of gender, ethnicity, where they come from or what their background may be. It is about creating a balanced mix of people on our teams and operating in an inclusive way in every part of our business, including the way we recruit, the way we market, create our products and the way we treat our customers. Social Innovation goes to a higher level and is a function that looks at how Toyota can be the very best it can be as

an employer, as a conscious operator, as a neighbor, and as a community partner.

We know that group think is one of the most dangerous things that can happen in large organizations. It leads to faulty assumptions and poor decision-making. The opposite of group think is an organization where creative ideas are brought up and lively debates occur at all levels. After those debates occur and decisions are made, there is no penalty or ill will from either side.

On a more tangible level, we know that 80% of vehicle purchases are influenced by women. Therefore, it is a business imperative that we hear women's perspectives in the way we design and market our vehicles. Toyota is doing just that, and our market share among female buyers is stronger than our overall market share. The same is true with African American, Hispanic, and Asian consumers. Another example is Toyota's annual innovation fair where team members at the grassroots level are encouraged to develop ideas to help the company save money, improve customer service, or enhance our corporate reputation.... It all ties back to Toyota's core principles of Respect for People and Continuous Improvement. Continuous improvement cannot happen without respect for people.

BARBARA WHYE was appointed Chief Diversity and Inclusion Officer and Vice President of Human Resources at Intel in 2017. She joined the company as an engineer in 1995 and moved steadily through various management positions. When we talked with her, you could tell she not only loves her job but truly believes in the company she works for. We learned, for example, that at Intel there's no longer any need to prove the value of inclusion as a component of business success. "When I'm asked to make the business case for diversity," she chuckles, "I say, 'You make the case for homogeneity.'"

Whye is straight forward and ready to showcase what works. She believes the first step in building inclusion is intentionality and commitment. Intel started by being transparent with data and reporting what was going on publicly, which had the effect of not only holding the company itself accountable but giving encouragement to others in the tech world. The company has long taken a leadership role on that front, investing $300 million to increase the presence of people of color and women in the industry and reach full representation in Intel's workforce by the year 2020, which it achieved two years earlier in 2018.

Internally, Intel incorporates inclusion in the measures used to determine employee bonuses. "What you measure matters," Whye argues. "This way we not only make clear our corporate intentions but make a solid case that every employee is involved." She also notes that she and her colleagues have come to realize that hiring is not enough; retention is crucial. "We cannot hire our way to success," she says. Hat's off to whomever, in 1995, had the foresight to hire her, and then create a corporate culture that harnesses the energy of Whye and many, many others also eager to achieve.

ROB BERNSHTEYN takes a holistic approach to the issue of inclusion, fitting both the issue itself and any strategies or tactics to achieve it within a clear definition of shared values. As CEO of Coupa, a Cloud Platform for Business Spend company named by *Fortune* in 2019 as one of the best workplaces in the San Francisco Bay Area, he points out that "it is a common set of values that makes an organization." In the case of Coupa, there are three such values, each (not surprisingly) phrased as an action:

to ensure customer success, to focus on results and to strive for excellence. Asked if in applying those values to, say, an interview process means making the hiring team itself inclusive, Bernshteyn says, "You know, I think it may be the reverse. We don't need to look for another one just like us."

KATE PURMAL gives new meaning to the phrase "been there, done that." In abbreviated form and chronological order, she: had a leadership role in the product development and marketing of Palm products, was CEO of a joint venture between SanDisk Corp. and M-Systems LTD, led a SanDisk start-up team to develop a new mobile video service and was CEO at Amnio Cure. Today she runs a consulting/coaching/advisory operation for CEOs and CTOs, as needed fills the role of interim COO or CFO and is Senior Industry Fellow at Georgetown University. Oh, and she and co-author Lisa Goldman have written an awarding-winning book: *The Moonshot Effect: Disrupting Business As Usual.* And still she took time to speak with us about her experiences with inclusion. Two of her perspectives are particularly cogent. First, she quite candidly suggests she has no real firsthand experience with any workplace that isn't inclusive. "Quite often, I have been the only woman in the room, but the very fact that I was there meant the group was not homogeneous," she points out. She adds, though, that in general "men are more willing to speak up than women," and that her daughter, who is bi-racial, is finding she is more comfortable in workplaces where there are others who are in some way "different." Second, moving from the experiential aspect to elements of business performance, Purmal stresses that she believes inclusive organizations will, by definition, hire the most talented people. Why? "Because, since they are the most talented, those people have their choice of jobs. Other things being equal, they will choose an inclusive culture. What's more, if they have accurately identified a culture in which they are more comfortable, they will stay longer."

LASZLO BOCK telegraphs just how different he is on his LinkedIn profile. As of this writing it reads: CEO and Co-founder of Humu. Author of *Work Rules!* Former SVP of People Operations at Google. Dad." A bit of elaboration on that is appropriate. First, the function of Humu, according to its website is to "make work better." How? By driving "behavioral change with the power of people science, machine learning—and love." Second, our favorite quote from *Work Rules!* is: "Culture eats strategy for breakfast." Third, during Bock's tenure at Google the company was named "Best Company to Work For" more than 30 times around the world. Fourth, Bock openly admits that his kids are his passion. As he puts it: "The biggest gift we can give the future is raising good people."[10]

When we interviewed Bock, he was completely honest about the fact that Google had put a great deal of effort into making both job applicants and employees comfortable, or as he puts it giving them "psychological safety." That requires, he suggests, more than one interview technique. What is easy for one may be daunting for another. Structured interviews are more appropriate for some; unstructured for others. And if an applicant does not comfortably speak English, then the interviewing team should include at least one person who speaks his/her language.

One particular technique Bock promotes is to give people at all levels of employment opportunities to "meet the people they are helping." As he writes in his book, "It imbues one's work with a significance that transcends careerism and money."[11]

ENDNOTES

1   Vivian Hunt, Dennis Layton and Sara Prince, "Diversity Matters," (McKinsey and Co., 2015), https://assets.mckinsey.com/~/media/ 857F440109AA4D13A54D9C496D86ED58.ashx.

2   Vivian Hunt, Sara Prince, Sundiatu Dixon-Fyle, and Lareina Yee, "Delivering through Diversity," (McKinsey and Co., 2018), https://www.mckinsey.com/~/media/mckinsey/business%20 functions/organization/our%20insights/delivering%20through%20diversity/delivering-through-diversity_full-report.ashx.

3   Ben Schiller, "Want at More Innovative Company? Simple: Hire a More Diverse Workforce," Fast Company, https://www.fastcompany.com/40515712/want-a-more-innovative-company-simple-hire-a-more-diverse-workforce.

4   Rocio Lorenzo, Nicole Voigt, Karin Schetelig, Annika Zawadzki, Isabeli Welpe, and Prisca Brosi, "The Mix That Matters: Innovation Through Diversity," (Boston Consulting Group and Technical University of Munich, 2017), http://media-publications.bcg.com/22feb2017-mix-that-matters.pdf.

5   Rebecca Riffkin and Jim Harter, "Using Employee Engagement to Build a Diverse Workforce," https://news.gallup.com/opinion/gallup/190103/using-employee-engagement-build-diverse-workforce.aspx.

6   Cindy Chen Delano, "Hedge Funds Have a Missed Opportunity that Could Be Hurting Results," https://www.barrons.com/articles/hedge-funds-gender-gap-could-be-hurting-performance-1543017569.

7   Andria Thomas, Joe Dougherty, Scott Strand, Abhinav Nayar and Maryam Janani, "Decoding Diversity: The Financial and Economic Returns to Diversity in Tech," (Intel and Dalberg Global Development Advisors, 2016) https://www.intel.com/content/www/us/en/diversity/decoding-diversity-report.html.

8   https://explorable.com/intergroup-discrimination.

9   Paolo Guardino, "Companies Should Stop Focusing on Diversity," https://www.forbes.com/sites/paologaudiano/2018/04/02/stop-focusing-on-diversity/#59f43be16764.

10 Meredith Bodgas, "Ex-Google Exec Powerfully Vindicates Working Mom Who Thinks She's Too into Her Kids," https://www.workingmother.com/ex-google-exec-powerfully-vindicates-working-mom-who-thinks-shes-too-into-her-kids.

11 Laszlo Bock, *Work Rules!* (New York: Twelve Books, 2015).

CHAPTER THREE

The Platform Is Burning

—

Many of us who work in the tech world have heard multiple times legendary computer scientist Alan Kay's maxim: "The best way to predict the future is to invent it." And the best way to get started on that invention is to accurately determine where one stands now. Unfortunately, all too many business leaders are so focused on quarterly reports, annual earnings, global competition, etc., that they fail to take a close look at trends that portend changes that will measurably—and perhaps disastrously—affect financial performance, growth and competitive advantage unless remediation begins now.

There are a number of forces at work when businesses and their leaders become content with the status quo. Here are three to consider:

1. **Complacency.** Two analogies, both relating to water, apply. The old proverb "The fish is the last to discover water" describes, of course, our tendency to fail to recognize our own environment. The familiar, because it's close and expected, becomes a given instead of an alternative. And unfortunately that persists even when the environment begins to change—as in the other proverb about the frog in water who fails to feel it getting hotter until he boils to death.

2. **Resistance to Change.** Harvard Business School professor Clayton Christensen received rave reviews for his no-nonsense book *The Innovator's Dilemma*,[1] in which he argues that in the face of innovation within a given market or

industry the practices that once made a business succeed could well become the practices that make it fail. His focus is technology, but the validity of his point assuredly is not confined to technological change.

3. **Mistaking Failure for Success.** Alan Perlis, the American computer scientist who was the first recipient of the Turing Award, famously wrote: "Dealing with failure is easy. Work hard to improve. Success is also easy. You've solved the wrong problem. Work hard to improve."[2] Many people may not be aware that it was a Kodak engineer who developed the first digital camera in 1975, but as he put it: "Management's reaction was 'That's cute, but don't tell anyone about it.' "[3] Corporate decision-makers feared its effect on the film industry. Kodak filed for bankruptcy in 2012. Similarly, in a 2013 *New Yorker* financial page column, James Surowuiecki described how Apple and Android had crushed Nokia in the smartphone business, because Nokia had become, in his words, "enthralled (and, in a way, imprisoned) by its past success."[4] Since at one time Nokia had earned more than half of all the profits in the mobile phone business, it failed to see the burgeoning popularity of smartphones. In contrast, wrote Surowuiecki, Apple executives recognized the value of both hardware and software and "encouraged employees to work in multidisciplinary teams to design products."

Now, a short analysis of how each of these three is playing out when it comes to the issue of inclusion.

Complacency: Many, if not most, successful businesses include verbiage in ads, on websites, in annual reports detailing their eagerness to make inclusion part of their core values. Often that may take the form of creating a place for a diversity officer on the management team. If that's all they do, it remains easy for such companies to overlook issues that could sound the death knell of business as they know it. Consider, for example:

- To grow, or even survive, do you need to extend your customer base to other demographic groups? If so, what do you know about their buying behavior?
- Is the communication among your employees comfortable enough to truly incubate emerging ideas from every organizational level?

Resistance to Change: In a 2012 *Financial Times* article,[5] John Kay argues that the kind of "resistance to innovative technology" that Christensen describes is at the core of why Sony failed to invent a viable alternative to the iPod—or better yet beat Apple to the punch. Indeed, he says, in companies like Sony change "threatens their existing capabilities and cannibalizes their existing products."

- Is maintaining the status quo in your company blinding you to the potentials offered by new technology, expanding markets, etc., because there is no one in a position to argue for change?
- Are you hiring new managers based on their experience in what your business does now or in what it could be doing three years from now?

Mistaking Failure for Success: In an intriguing analysis of how to detect bias,[6] essayist Paul Graham points out that if applicants of one type—let's say Indonesian—have to perform better than other applicants to be chosen, the Indonesians who make it through can be expected to outperform others selected at the same time. For that reason, he suggests, when First Round Capital at one point reported that startups with female founders among its portfolio companies outperformed those without female founders by a rousing 63 percent, by limiting the sample to their own portfolio they were actually (and in all likelihood unwittingly) describing a study not of startup trends but of their own bias in selecting companies.

- At the 1997 Apple Worldwide Developers' Conference, Steve Jobs said companies need to prioritize their customers' experience, and work back from that.[7] If you're doing that, will it lock you into the profile of current customers? Can your products sell to customers who prefer another type experience?
- When strategizing based on positive macroeconomic indicators, do you take into account the fact that the GDP has come to describe the affluent and not the total population, to the point that a group of academicians has started publishing an alternative version? And, did you remember that adults who are looking for work, but cannot find jobs, even though they are not working, not going to school and not taking care of children are also not counted in the official US unemployment rate?

THE NUMBERS, PLEASE

A look at where US businesses actually stand on measures of inclusion across industries shows definitively that for a good number of companies, **the platform is burning.**

- There are more corporate CEOs named "John" or "David" in the US than there are female CEOs.[8]
- Employers are less likely to call applicants who submit resumes with African-American-sounding names than those with Caucasian-sounding names.[9] (*University of Wisconsin*)

- When Microsoft was developing Clippy, its paperclip office assistant (remember that?), it spent $100,000 on market testing, then ignored female responses that the characters were too male—90 percent of them.[10]
- Men are 30 percent more likely than women to be promoted from entry level to manager (*Women in the Workplace*).[11]
- In the nonprofit world, seven in ten leaders consider inclusion an important goal, but only 36 percent believe they've achieved it (*Center for Effective Philanthropy*).[12] And while nine out of ten of the board members of nonprofits insist inclusion is critical to success, fewer than half of them have taken any action to change the composition of their own membership.[13]
- Among the CEOs of *Fortune* 500 companies in 2018, there are only 24 females, down from 32 the year before (the highest percentage in history).[14] Among the S&P 500, the number was one less—23 in 2018, but 26 in 2019.[15]
- The picture for African-Americans is bleaker still, at only three the lowest number since 2002 (*Fortune*).[16]

It is important to remember, too, that these trends and the reaction to them are not exclusive to the United States economy. But there are exceptions. Gianfranco Ferrari, CEO of Banco de Credito del Peru BCP, in our interview with him describes what the bank is doing to address and incorporate current and anticipated changes:

> Banking no longer seeks the typical banker. We now actively recruit psychologists, mathematicians, data scientists, statisticians, designers...not necessarily looking the same as the typical profile of a banker.... That is why...we have been working on a major change in the value proposition for the employee.... Today we are implementing agility across the

bank, working in squads and tribes in a completely different layout from a few years ago.... I am convinced this is a change that will not stop, and in that sense we will continue adapting to it in the future.

By failing to prepare,
you are preparing to fail.

~ Benjamin Franklin

PERSPECTIVES ON POINT

Insights Gained from Personal Interviews by the Authors

ALEXANDER COWARD is a man who succeeded in one system and used that success to improve the system in a way that sounds for all the world like he rejected it. Having grown up in inner-city London, he spent ten years at Oxford, earning an undergraduate degree and teaching credentials before completing his doctorate in mathematics in 2008, specializing in topology and geometry in three dimensions. Having lived in Australia and Vietnam (where he was awarded an honorary doctorate by Thai Nguyen University), he also taught on two different campuses of the University of California system before founding EDeeU Education, an education company that combines independent learning with seminars and community events facilitated by what is called a "Director of Studies." Since the idea is to take advantage of resources such as other online information aggregators and libraries, the EDeeU experience is affordable. The group of directors is inclusionary in every way but one: all have credentials from recognized universities if they are academicians or demonstrated success in whatever field they are working if not.

Coward believes there is one hard and fast rule to avoid any chance that the platform will burn, and that is to begin at the beginning. "The shape of the seed determines the shape of the tree," he argues. "If you want your program, your project, your company to be inclusionary, you cannot say you will 'do that later.' If at the end of the first year, you're surrounded by a monoculture, changing that is a big deal. Inclusion must be part of the original design."

JEFF YASUDA is CEO and Founder of Feed.fm, which provides customers—like Fitbit, American Eagle Outfitters and Nautilus, to name only three—special media solutions to drive commerce, increase app retention rates and measurably ratchet up visit-to-purchase conversion. With an undergraduate degree in history, an MBA in finance and accounting, and a CPA, he clearly has the desire to recognize creative excellence and the discipline to identify effective applications and distribution methods. Not surprisingly, perhaps, his take on inclusion has to do not only with the standard issues of gender and ethnicity, but with diversity of thought. And, he points out that traditionally sources of funding for startups have been derived from either family wealth or the venture capital world, both of which are almost by definition homogeneous. More recently, bootstrapping has taken hold and nontraditional sources have been tapped—again innovative thinking—so that the situation has begun to change. It is worth noting that Yasuda's personal style of inclusion has been described by one of his colleagues writing on his LinkedIn page this way: "I watched Jeff take an idea and turn it into a reality greater than anyone imagined. His willingness to try others' ideas and give them room to become their best is unmatched in my experience as an employee."

YOSEN UTOMO left his native Indonesia to study in this country a decade ago. He and Ed Ow, a friend he met when they were both students at UC Berkeley, cofounded Fulldive VR, a virtual reality platform that is based on a smartphone. Both men are eager to create a product that will not only be accessible not only to those with limited incomes in this country, but also in portions of the Third World where many people have no real access to technology beyond a cellphone. It would probably be fair to say that Utomo has fewer "thoughts" about inclusion than he does experiences. He sums it up in one question and answer: "Why is Silicon Valley the most innovative place on earth? Because our talent comes from 130+ countries." That reality is a good bit more than virtual.

MARIAN ZIZZO NAZAR has spent much of her professional life working in various roles and with multiple organizations to help them identify and hire what she describes as "mission-driven talent" to nurture and enrich the social impact of the companies and their leaders. She has been involved with collaborations that are both national and international, profit and nonprofit, very large (e.g., The World Bank) and small, corporate and individual. When our interviews took place, she was active in the Tech Inclusion Initiative powered by Change Catalyst, which staged events throughout the world taking an ecosystem approach to inclusion issues, rather than one specific to a particular sector. As part of her work she developed panel discussions involving corporate representatives, educators, policymakers, investors and entrepreneurs

Her take on the issue of inclusion is that it requires close attention and rigorous application, because implicit bias is all but ubiquitous. She points out that even artificial intelligence can be biased, depending on who writes the code and how the algorithms seek and distribute data. To support her argument quite simply, she recalls an incident when she was shopping, picked up a skincare product and began to read the label. This particular product, the label specified, was for "normal to darker" skin. Who decided what was normal? she wondered.

Nazar calls particular attention to the crucial part that inclusion plays in employee retention. As she puts it, what much of Western society refers to as the "Golden Rule" as in treat others as you would like to be treated has now become treat others as *they* would like to be treated.

BILL COLEMAN, who was still serving as CEO of Veritas Technologies LLC when we conducted our interview, is now Operating Executive at the Carlyle Group, as well as special partner at Virtuvian Partners and Venture Partner at Alsop Louie Partners. His leadership skills and experience in founding businesses, staging turnarounds and articulating strategy to elicit employee buy-in are legendary. On the subject of inclusion, he is at once practical and visionary. There is no way to achieve results, he insists, unless you "live it, walk it, talk about it" until it becomes real and an essential part of the organizational culture. And the second step is to be proactive in every conceivable way with/about all groups, not only among employees but within the community as well.

DAN SCHULMAN became the President and CEO of Paypal when it split from eBay in 2015, bringing with him a wealth of experience in the financial world and in mobile technology. His experience early in his career as President and CEO at Priceline was followed by nearly two decades at AT&T including a stint as President of the Consumer Markets Division, which led to his founding Virgin Mobile USA. When that company was acquired by Sprint Nextel Corporation, he became the President of Prepaid Group there, then served as Group President of Enterprise Growth at American Express. It seems almost lame to say "he knows his business," but he does, and he's passionate about the value of inclusion. As he sees it, inclusion "should not be an objective in and of itself, but part of a creative vision and mission that is inspiring, and therefore naturally inclusive, enough to appeal to the best and the brightest." He insists that at Paypal it is a core value, which means it is more than intellectually understood. It is internalized. It meshes with the corporate mission of Paypal, which he describes as "democratization of financial services, since moving money should be the right of every citizen in every country."

While others sometimes describe diversity as "diversity of thought" (and still others suggest that definition can itself be a way of avoiding the challenges of including marginalized groups), Schulman sees diversity of thought as a *result* of inclusion, and a crucial result at that. "The greatest competitive advantage a company has is its ability to attract and keep talent. When there are different points of view represented and the people in the room feel as if they belong, customers will be better served, which means that shareholders will be, too," he says.

Schulman had lots of opportunities to express those values in 2019, when his company reported it had not only closed a $3-million pay gap in record time, but to make sure such a gap did not recur had instituted a program based on not only performance, but job title, years of experience and location, with any subjective evaluations informed by outside consultants.

MITCH BARNS had served Nielsen Company in multiple roles and multiple countries over a period of 15-plus years before he took over as CEO in 2014, so it was an organization he understood well. Yet based on that experience, he believed that the time had come to take a hard look at what the future might bring and how Nielsen could walk boldly into that future. "I remember hearing an MIT professor, Lester Thurow, say, 'the most difficult time to change is in the absence of a crisis.'" Since the standard business indicators at Nielsen were sound when he took the lead, his idea of moving away from a professional services model to one that maximized the power of technology toward a data-as-a-service model was not an easy decision. During his five years at the helm, digital revenues tripled, emerging markets increased 50 percent and total revenues 25 percent on a constant currency basis. As he reflects on his experience, he makes several cogent points:

- Projection is crucial. "Today is today. You've got to look to tomorrow." (For Nielsen, that meant seeing how Netflix and others like it would change the entertainment/media/advertising landscape.)
- To get buy-in, "simplification works best."
- "The strategy you execute is the one the company depends on, not the one that looks good in a Power Point presentation."

SILVINA MOSCHINI has a well-earned reputation for leadership in meshing technological applications and solutions with corporate employment practices and policies for an outcome that not only faces the future but helps form it. She is Co-founder of Transparent Business, a web-based solution to issues surrounding recruiting and managing freelance talent, and from that developed SheWorks to help clients such as Google, Microsoft and Facebook engage online education and flexibility in their use of time and space in ways that will empower women. She is clear that her own success derives from innovative leadership. As she puts it:

There is no easy road to being an entrepreneur: it takes passion, grit, determination, and perseverance. When you are bringing a new concept to the table that changes the rules and breaks free of the "norm," it's an uphill battle, facing roadblocks that make it difficult to find initial supporters and investors. Most people can appreciate innovation, but when the time comes to change, and "walk your talk," most will revert to traditional systems and rules. I have been so fortunate to have had a valuable network of key leaders, advisors, and investors who embrace change, driving diversity and inclusion for the future of work.

JENNIFER HOPP describes herself as an "investor, advisor and entrepreneur," which is accurate but hardly the complete story. She currently is involved in three ventures based in San Juan, Puerto Rico: ATO Ventures, a VC tech fund; BizStart Live, a livestream broadcast service to connect startups and investors; and Emvy, a market validation testing service. And that does not count the various firms that seek her advice. Having recently moved to Puerto Rico, she is keenly aware of the importance of what might be called "cultural consciousness." As she tells us:

> At ATO Ventures, our team is small, but incredibly diverse. Gender, race and cultural differences abound, yet these pale in comparison to our diversity of thought. Contrasting perspectives have been formed from a wide array of experience and cultures and represent everything from Christian to atheist, wealthy to poor, politically right to extreme left, and hyper-optimist to perpetual pessimist.

She goes on to add that one of the team members is particularly adept at understanding the political factions in the country, which is invaluable for investors seeking to navigate a culture with "a deep history of political conflict." Important? Indeed. "The startup scene in Puerto Rico is on fire," she says. "The energy is palpable and the speed at which we are growing dictates that this is our game to lose."

ROSHAWNNA NOVELLUS should meet Malcolm Gladwell, if she hasn't already. (We neglected to ask, but we might just ask her if we can send him a book with a bookmark tucked in front of this page.) Why? Because hers is the kind of story he chronicles. It would take a good bit more space than we have to describe it totally here, so we'll just provide three teasers:

1. At the age of 15, Novellus decided she didn't want her mother to worry about paying for her education, asked for some stationery and stamps, wrote letters to 200 addressees (not people or organizations she necessarily had had any contact with) and raised $600,000. This was before the term "crowdfunding" had even been coined.

2. She believes in multiples: degrees—BS, BA, MS, DSc, all earned Summa cum Laude; business ventures that help business venturers—EnrichHER, TechStars, TheWealthyYogi.com, Bootstrap Capital, and those are just the current ones; and never giving up—that $600,000 we just described, weeks at an ashram in Thailand to help identify what she is about, climbing through swirls of red tape to actualize whatever venture will serve her purpose.

3. She has a Gladwell-like ability to focus on the side of issues often either overlooked or under-appreciated.

"You know," Novellus muses, "the notion of access and support for the under-represented groups of thought leaders, such as women, is all too often something people just talk about, and fail to do anything about. Doing something about it means shattering the glass ceiling."

Interestingly, in seeking funding for her own businesses, Novellus points out there are three approaches, each viable in its own way. "You can go to the ones who have a history of this kind of investment, you can go to those who don't and argue that it would be good for their image, or you can simply point to the expected success, and appeal to those who know a winner when they see it."

COCO BROWN is the CEO & Founder of Athena Alliance, a digitally based, curated ecosystem that is revolutionizing leadership development and access. Athena's mission is to ensure all leaders— entrepreneurs, investors, executives and board directors—operate at their highest levels of impact. Women gain access to power networks that ensure they are in the right place at the right time for a variety of business opportunities. And, investors, companies, and boards gain access to top women in business.

Based on her experience, Brown asserts that in American business, the new normal is becoming a state of fluidity, and what that means is:

- change and differences are prized;
- embracing and leveraging diversity enables a vastly greater ability to adapt to change; and
- the ability to rapidly change and adapt is a key to competitive advantage.

As she explains it:

We're realizing diversity is key to success. As equals in today's economy, women now make up half the workforce as well as half the household breadwinners. What's more they make 83 percent of the buying decisions, including in situations heretofore considered the domain of men. For example, women make the decision 65 percent of the time for the purchase of a car, 89 percent of time regarding financial services and 80 percent of healthcare decisions.

That said, women remain under-represented in the corporate world. Only 29 percent of vice presidents, 21 percent of senior vice presidents and 21 percent of C Suite executives across all industries and business sizes are female, representing a growth of only 6 percent, 1 percent and 4 percent respectively in the last four years.

Women have traditionally held leadership roles that focus more on people and connection to people, and far fewer of the top roles in product, finance and sales. And, interestingly, the roles American corporate structures traditionally put closest to the CEO are those male-dominated roles. But, with the increasing power of the consumer, and the rise of a connected society whose voice carries tremendous weight and consequence, this is changing. And this is good for women.

As culture and market oversight, organizational design and people risk begin to take front seats in leadership domains, so will women. Already, women represent:

- 55 percent of chief human resource officers
- 35 percent of chief compliance officers
- 35 percent of chief medical officers
- 32 percent of chief marketing officers
- 19 percent of chief information officers and chief technology officers.

ENDNOTES

[1] Clayton M. Christensen, *The Innovator's Dilemma: When New Technologies Cause Great Firms to Fail*, (Brighton, MA: Harvard Business School Press, 1997) pdfs.semanticscholar.org/1b9c/8b37c8d28398f094582add71f65eec1cad1d.pdf.

[2] www.goodreads.com/quotes/626607-dealing-with-failure-is-easy-work-hard-to-improve-success.

[3] Chunka Mui, "How Kodak Failed," www.forbes.com/sites/chunkamui/2012/01/18/how-kodak-failed/#14c773a36f27.

[4] James Surowiecki, "Where Nokia Went Wrong," www.newyorker.com/business/currency/where-norkia-wnet-wrong.

[5] John Kay, "Why Sony Did Not Invent the Ipod: Industries with the power to hold back economic growth open the door to outsiders," www.ft.com/content/7558a99e-f5ed-11e1-a6c2-00144feabdc0.

[6] Paul Graham, "The Way to Detect Bias," www.paulgraham.com/bias.html.

[7] Darmesh Shah, "16 Brilliant Insights from Steve Jobs Keynote Circa 1997," www.onstartups.com/tabid/3339/bid/58082/16-Brilliant-Insights-From-Steve-Jobs-Keynote-Circa-1997.aspx.

[8] Claire Cain Miller, Kevin Quealy and Margot Sanger-Katz, "The Top Jobs Where Women Are Outnumbered by Men Named John," www.nytimes.com/interactive/2018/04/24/upshot/women-and-men-named-john.html.

[9] Eve Fine and Jo Handelsman, "Reviewing Applicants: Research on Bias and Assumptions," (Madison, WI: Women in Science and Engineering Institute, University of Wisconsin, Madison) https://wiseli.wisc.edu/wp-content/uploads/sites/662/2018/10/BiasBrochure_3rdEd.pdf.

[10] Abigail Cain, "The Life and Death of Microsoft Clippy, the Paper Clip the World Loved to Hate," www.artsy.net/article/artsy-editorial-life-death-microsoft-clippy-paper-clip-loved-hate.

[11] Rachel Thomas, Marianne Cooper, PhD, Ellan Konar, PhD, Megan Rooney, Mary Noble-Tolla, PhD, Ali Bohrer, Lareina Ye, Alexis Krivkovich, Irina Starikova, Kelsey Robinson, Marie-Claude Hadeau, and Nicole Robinson, PhD, "Women in the Workplace 2018," (LeanIn and McKinsey and Co., 2018) https://womenintheworkplace.com/.

[12] Ben Paynter, "Non-Profits Know They Need to Get More Diverse—but They Aren't," www.fastcompany.com/90206257/nonprofits-know-they-need-to-get-more-diverse-but-they-arent.

[13] Ben Paynter, "The People Running Non-Profits Continue to Be Rich, White, and Unsure How to Change That," www.fastcompany.com/90297272/the-people-running-nonprofits-continue-to-be-rich-white-and-unsure-how-to-change-that.

[14] Zameena Mejia, "Just 24 Female CEOs Lead the Compnies on the 2018 Fortune 500—Fewer Than Last Year," www.cnbc.com/2018/05/21/2018s-fortune-500-companies-have-just-24-female-ceos.html.

[15] www.catalyst.org/research/women-ceos-of-the-sp-500/.

[16] Grace Donnelly, "The Number of Black CEOs at Fortune 500 Companies Is at Its Lowest Since 2002," http://fortune.com/2018/02/28/black-history-month-black-ceos-fortune-500/.

CHAPTER FOUR

The Changing of the Guard: Evolving Demographics

—

In a commentary he wrote for *The Globe and Mail* in 2017,[1] Mark Milke, president of the Sir Winston Churchill Society of Calgary, offered a thorough analysis of why Sears Canada was failing. He suggested a formula he called "the three I's"—the right ideas, individuals and aligned interests. As he explained it: "Sears failed because apparently no one in the executive suite or at the board level had the right ideas about the new retail environment; that means for some time Sears was led by the wrong individuals."

At first, that sounds like a call for corner-suite/boardroom housecleaning. But a better approach involves two elements: (1) the right "mixture"; and (2) informing and convincing the existing individuals about what lies ahead. Both may well depend for their success on inclusion.

Customer surveys, even the most statistically valid ones, more often than not measure the opinions of the individuals surveyed, not their knowledge. And if those opinions derive only from experiences, they are by definition limited. As Henry Ford is so often quoted as saying: "If I had asked people what they wanted, they would have said faster horses."

Inventing the future, as discussed in the last chapter, is successful when planning focuses on what is to be, not what is now. A leadership team that features a collection of creative minds, representing a broad array of cultural backgrounds, business experiences and specific skill sets, can exhibit the kind of strength that does not have to look for the light at the end of the tunnel because it can find the way around the tunnel.

Social scientists and business consultants alike see radical demographic changes ahead for the United States.

From Age to Age

On the population front, according to the US Census Bureau March 2018 report:[2]

- In 2016 roughly 15 percent of the population was 65 or older. By 2060, that number will be 23 percent. In raw numbers, that means nearly double: 49 million to 95 million. That would produce a United States that is much like Japan is today, but still one that does not face as serious an aging phenomenon as Japan, Canada, Germany, Italy, France and Spain.
- Among that older segment, women will still outnumber men, but less so. In 2016, there were 79 men for 100 women in the US over 65. In 2060, the projected number of men is 86.
- While the levels of immigration are projected to stay relatively flat, because of the aging of the population death rates will outpace birthrates and the proportion of population growth attributed to immigration will rise. What's more, foreign-born residents typically experience lower mortality rates and longer life expectancy than native-born Americans, and the foreign-born women have slightly more children. Yes, this will push the percentage of foreign-born up from today's 14 percent to 17 percent in 2060.

There has been more than a little brouhaha over projections that have been erroneously reported to suggest that within the near future Hispanics will outnumber whites. Not so. What is happening, as William H. Frey, senior fellow at the Brookings Institution analyzes the data,[3] is that beginning in 2045:

- Whites, at 40.7 percent, will no longer constitute the majority of the population. The remainder is divided into 24.6 percent Hispanic, 13.1 percent black, 7.9 percent Asian, and 3.8 percent multiracial.

- Two trends are at work here, explains Frey: (1) By 2060 the racial minority populations will have grown by 74 percent (from 2018); and (2) the aging white population, which will continue to grow through 2024, will then begin a long decline as deaths outpace births.

Of special importance in Frey's analysis is the fact that the tipping point varies significantly by age, to the point that for those under 18, minorities will outnumber whites in 2020. By 2060, the Census projects, whites will constitute just over one-third of the under-18 population.

At roughly the same time the Census Report was issued in 2018, the Pew Research Center identified seven demographic trends that are expected to create significant change.[4] Three of those could especially affect how business leaders should plan:

- Twenty percent, a record number, of Americans live in multi-generational households.

- At one time there was essentially no difference in Americans' level of education based on marital status. Now, half of those with a high school degree and no college are married; 55 percent with some post-high school education are married, and 65 percent of the college-educated are married.

- Millennials (those born between 1981 and 1996), who already make up more than a third of the labor force, will surpass Baby Boomers as the largest population segment in the US in 2019.

Interestingly, a generational study that is part of the Goldman Sachs *What If I Told You* series[5] includes a comparison of Millennials and Generation Zers, the oldest of whom were born in 1998, and (according to Bloomberg Research) will outnumber the Millennials beginning in 2019. Goldman Sachs Research Analyst Christopher Wolf quotes Census Bureau statistics when he forecasts that by next year more than half the children in America will belong to a non-White or ethnic group.

The Gen Z characteristics the Goldman Sachs study posits that are of particular interest to the business community are:

- In fashion, a preference for the bland, basic—sometimes called "Nomcore" or "Normcore"—with no need to stand out by wearing a specific brand.
- Fiscally conservative
- More conscious of protecting their reputation online than Millennials
- Entrepreneurial
- Adept at online shopping, which when combined with their fiscal point of view makes for a taste for the best deal.

John Wang, Founder and President of the Asian American Business Development Center, writing for the *Huffington Post* "What's Working: Purpose + Profit platform,"[6] adds that Gen Z will be the most racially diverse group ever. In fact—again according to the US Census Bureau—2020 will see just over half of children under 18 coming from a "minority" race or ethnic group. He adds that, also in 2020, Gen Zers will account for 30 percent of the work force and 40 percent of the consumer market, with spending power amounting to more than $100 billion.

THE THREE-POINT PLANNING POLL

Customers: A Canvas8 study of consumer trends in 2019[7] concludes the younger complement will be:

- More self-expressive, less into conformity on the fashion/beauty front.
- Focused on responsible consumerism
- Into healthy eating
- Perhaps leaning toward a combination of physical and digital in shopping experiences, based on a preference to actually "hold products" and a concern for the waste generated by online shopping

These are only a few of the predicted changes. How can you adjust products and services to meet the expectations of Millennials and the up and coming Gen Zers if no one in a decision-making capacity understands them? Better yet, how can you *drive* those expectations if some of these age groups aren't part of the team in the lead?

Work Environments: In its 2019 report on the future workforce, Upwork[8] found more than half the Millennial/Gen Z managers see workforce planning as a top priority, and this group is twice as likely as boomers to translate that into more flexible iterations, such as remote and freelance. Are you ready?

Employee Training: In a 2019 report, the World Economic Forum,[9] in collaboration with the Boston Consulting Group, predicted that the 1.37 million workers in the US expected to be displaced by artificial intelligence and other advances according to the Bureau of Labor Statistics could be reskilled to new and higher-wage positions for roughly $24,800 each. Are these likely to be skewed toward one age group? Are you ready? [The top declining jobs include such positions as secretaries and administrative assistants (except in executive, legal and medical settings), cashiers, production line employees, bookkeeping, accounting and auditing clerks, etc.]

Is it a bit foolish to lump all non-white cultures into one customer profile, especially now that those cultures represent *more* of the total population than the white group? What information do you need and how will you get it to appropriately include different perspectives and buying habits?

Immigration Myths and Modalities

In 2017, the Center for American Entrepreneurship took a look at the Fortune 500 companies[10] for that year and found that more than half of the top 35 were founded by an immigrant or the child of an immigrant. Of the full list of 500, 216 met that criterion and accounted for 12.1 million workers worldwide and $5.3 trillion in global revenue. Perhaps the most compelling message derived from those numbers was expressed by Ian Hathaway, writing for the Brookings Institution:[11]

> Though accounting for less than 14 percent of the population, immigrants found almost a quarter of all new businesses, nearly one-third of venture-backed companies, and half of Silicon Valley high-tech startups.

Many foreign-born founders of iconic American companies—those in the Fortune 500—were poor, young, and fleeing harsh economic and political conditions. A recent Harvard Business School study found that among foreign-born entrepreneurs, those who come here as children have among the best business outcomes (growth and survival rates).

So, we can rest easy. The skills and talents of immigrants as employees and their potential buying power are being adequately recognized. Hardly. (More on this, though, in Chapter 5.) A 2017 *Forbes* article[12] cited a Nerdwallet analysis of household earning power that showed that in 45 states immigrants were making less money than their US citizen counterparts.

Perhaps because the 2019 US political climate is rife with counter claims involving the need for a reinforced southern border, as this book is being written Hispanics tend to draw more fire than others among the foreign-born. Interestingly, by 2017, only 34.4 percent of Hispanics in the US were immigrants, according to Pew Research.[13] Whether foreign-born or not, though, Hispanics constitute an important market, especially since they represent a large complement of the younger potential customers and employees. Parker Morse, the CEO of H Code Media, offers some relevant statistics:[14]

- Roughly one in four children under age 9 in the US are Hispanic.
- Annual brand marketing on TV to Hispanics tops $6 billion.
- Hispanics spend more time on mobile devices than does the rest of the population, and are also more likely to use streaming platforms on those devices.
- Nearly half the Hispanic Millennials say they talk about brands online with others or use the brands' hashtags compared to 17 percent of non-Hispanics.

> We know from an ethnicity perspective today's kindergarteners entering Silicon Valley public schools are more than 50 percent Latino.
>
> ~ Carl Guardino | President and CEO, Silicon Valley Leadership Group

In an article published in *Inc.* Magazine, Michael A. Olguin, President of Havas Formula PR,[15] provides a qualitative research perspective, describing Hispanics as quite loyal to their friends, family and beliefs. Companies interested in their $1.7 trillion in purchasing power, expected to rise to $1.9 trillion by 2022, will take note of that.

THE THREE-POINT PLANNING POLL

Customers: It is a common practice among Americans to lump together various cultures under one label. Just as there are measured (and sometimes treasured) differences between an American who grew up in Oklahoma and one who grew up in Oregon, so too are there substantial differences between a Mexican-American and a Peruvian-American, both categorized as "Hispanic." Similarly, while sharing a language is important, it is rarely enough. Indeed, Hispanics report that they are more likely to engage online in English if their mission is commercial instead of personal. Early on, in citing the McKinsey study regarding the effects of inclusion—abbreviated reminder: EBIT rises 8 percent for every 10 percent increase in the rate of racial and ethnic diversity at the senior executive level and ethnically diverse companies can be expected to be more likely to outperform their industry-based medians by 35 percent—we noted that this may not presuppose direct causality. What can be safely argued is that an inclusionary company has done the work to determine precisely what kinds of inclusion, how widespread and on what levels are important. Have you?

The stats pretty much speak for themselves: the Hispanic consumer marketplace is growing in numbers, regions, and influence.

Any brand ignoring this would be foolish. As Michael Olquin put it: "When I was growing up my Mexican-American mother used to tell me, 'It's important to love both cultures.'" Brands would be wise to follow the same advice and, when developing marketing programs, think beyond the general market to consider what could or should be done to connect with Hispanic audiences.[16]

Work Environments: Latinos and Latinas responding to a *Harvard Business Review* study in 2016[17] insisted they felt it necessary to repress their natural personalities—be less emotional, use their hands less, dress and behave in ways that are cohesive with an "executive presence." These same individuals begin to believe their ideas, also, are not welcomed and valued. Perhaps the most dramatic issue in recent years in work environments has involved Muslim women who choose to wear a headscarf. In 2017, Tasneem Afridi, who grew up in Pakistan, began production of a YouTube series that dealt with her experiences as a hijabi. She received a YouTube Creators for Change fellowship for her work. In a piece written for refinery29.com,[18] she notes that she is happy to have the opportunity to discuss her background and beliefs with her colleagues and has never experienced blatant workplace discrimination, but says she is subject to what she calls "micro-aggressions" in and out of the workplace. Trying to contain her emotional reactions when her faith does come up at work, she maintains that "It is not appropriate to single people out, especially in a professional setting." And in your corporate offices, how would she fare?

Employee Training: There are, of course, a wide variety of firms offering employee training on inclusion and diversity, but as a *Harvard Business Review* research paper published in 2017[19] points out, there is also lack of consensus on whether or not training is effective, and some suggest it may even create backlash. The researchers concurred that the success of training can differ significantly, but from their experiments recommended what they termed "perspective-taking," which they define as "mentally walking in someone else's shoes." They had their subjects write a few sentences describing how a particular marginalized group might feel, and then tested the subjects' attitude about *another* minority, discovering they showed more positive attitudes and behaviors. (In a follow-up report a year later, however, results of another research project revealed that perspective-taking fails to increase one's understanding of what others want.)[20] A second method their research proved to be effective is goal-setting, which means setting goals having to do with inclusion that are specific, measurable and difficult to attain. Who in your organization could be tasked to develop and execute this kind of training?

Sexishly Speaking

Today, there is limited utility in presenting statistics to verify the wage gap between men and women in the US. Few argue that it exists; but some continue to insist it either doesn't matter or is justified. The same divided attitude applies to defining the appropriate number of women in the workforce: Equal to the percentage in the employable portion of the population? Equal to the percentage of those adequately trained for the position? Defined by industry-based factors?

In a comprehensive 2018 report entitled "Women in the Workplace" [21] LeanIn and McKinsey&Company treat these and other issues, finding that:

- The underrepresentation of women is *not* due to attrition; they are left behind from the beginning.
- Receiving less support from managers and having less access to senior leaders, women feel it is more difficult for them to advance and that the workplace is not, after all, fair.
- Sexual harassment is still prevalent.

- The researchers suggest six actions companies might take. Test your company on these:
    1. Start with the basics and get them right—targets... accountability...reporting.
    2. Make sure hiring and promotions are fair across the board.
    3. Set your senior leaders and managers up to be champions of diversity.
    4. Work to make your corporate culture inclusive and respectful.
    5. Limit or eliminate instances when a woman is the "only woman."
    6. Offer your employees the flexibility to fit their work with you into their lives.

All of these, of course, derive from making gender inclusion a priority. The benefits, say the McKinsey authors, are proven: "new ideas, better results, and happier employees."

THE THREE-POINT PLANNING POLL

Customers: Emily Chang, in her book entitled *BROTOPIA: Breaking Up the Boys Club of Silicon Valley,*[22] provides a particularly relevant case study on how the employment of females can quickly change customer acceptance and use of a product or service. The company is Redfin, a real estate technology company founded in 2004 and based in Seattle. It was having difficulty getting its agents to use a particular software that automated house tour schedules. When more female engineers had been hired, the developers decided to visit some of the agents (more than half of whom were female and many without college degrees) before they proceeded with any more development. That visit prompted a reworking of the product, which in turn tripled adoption and generated an extra $30 million in revenue over 18 months. What questions should you be asking and who should ask them?

Work Environments: The six points above apply here, but they, too, can be enhanced by the Redfin experience. When a woman named Bridget Frey was promoted to chief technology officer, she started to do things that would build a system of fairness. At the same time, she recruited for engineering positions women with nontraditional backgrounds, moving some from the Redfin marketing team. And did they perform as well as their computer-science graduate counterparts? They were promoted at about the same rate.

Employee Training: Focus one more time on the six points above, and then—again—here's what Frey has to say about the Redfin experience. Conflict, she maintains, can be a good thing so long as you teach people how to deal with it and remain open to making mistakes. She admits that when it comes to inclusion best practices are still evolving, so there will be awkward moments. Crucial to the process is keeping all workers educated on what you're trying to do, having the data to justify your initiatives, and remaining ready to talk openly about how the process is proceeding.

Tony West, whose career has spanned legal positions with PepsiCo and Uber as well as his work as Assistant US Attorney General, insists that the issue of inclusion is "not rocket science." As he explains further: "This is not a complex issue. It is all about being intentional...mindful, if you will."

Who's What

Originally a reasonably simple social "taxonomy," the custom of sorting people born since the beginning of the 20th century into "generations" with labels and distinctive characteristics has become a bit messy as different researchers fail to concur on dates and add descriptors that may or may not have been verified with sufficient research. Still, a brief overview can help individuals and organizations working on inclusion issues identify pressure points. As usual, dates refer to birth years, and it is important to remember that no matter what the source, generational descriptions can become what is referred to in advertising and liberally used in propaganda as "glittering generalities," not to mention stereotypes.

GI 1901 TO 1924 – Tom Brokaw's *The Greatest Generation*
> *At work:* respect authority, follow the rules, get it done right, be loyal
> *Leadership style:* directive, authoritative, formal
> *Family:* traditional nuclear, stay-at-home moms
> *What we want:* financial security, health care, human contact

SILENT 1925 TO 1945 – also sometimes combined with GI
and referred to as the Veterans or Traditionalists
> *At work:* respect authority, follow the rules, get it done right
> *Leadership style:* directive, authoritative, formal
> *Family:* traditional nuclear, stay-at-home moms, but some war-based female employment
> *What we want:* respect for experience, organizational loyalty

BABY BOOMERS 1946 TO 1964

At work: emphasize quality, work efficiently and as long as it takes

Leadership style: collegial, team player, likes meetings, sometimes not supportive of flexibility

Family: traditional nuclear, but affected by WWII-generated value changes

Technology: use for productivity, mixed on comfort level

What we want: to be valued for contributions

GENERATION X 1965 TO 1979 – also the Sandwich Generation

At work: look for structure and direction, but remain skeptical; embrace change; tech pioneers; entrepreneurial

Leadership style: egalitarian and fair, but willing to challenge others and ask "why"; self-reliant

Family: latch-key kids

What we want: schedule flexibility, life/work balance

MILLENNIALS 1980 TO 2000 – once also Generation Y and Me Generation

At work: entrepreneurial, use work for fulfillment, goal-oriented, embrace inclusion

Leadership style: feel pressure to be successful, tech-focus can negatively affect interpersonal skills;

Family: merged, increased parental coaching

What we want: flexibility, the opportunity to work with bright people and innovate

GENERATION Z 2001 TO 2013

At work: respect authority, follow the rules, get it done right, heavily entrepreneurial

Leadership style: directive, authoritative, but also cautious

Family: non-traditional, same-gender, non-marital

What we want: TBD

All sources post 2010, and include but are not limited to: www.kepner-tregoe.com/blog/critical-thinking-spanning-the-generations; www.fdu.edu/newspubs/magazine/05ws/generations.html; https://www.businessinsider.com/au/hw-millennials-gen-x-and-boomers-shape-the-workplace-2013-9; www.psychologytoday.com/us/blog/the-truisms-wellness/201602/baby-boomers-generation-z; www.npr.org/2014/10/06/349316543/don-t-label-me-origins-of-generational-names-and-why-we-use-them; www.npr.org/2014/11/18/354196302/amid-the-stereotypes-some-facts-about-millennials; www.theatlantic.com/sponsored/goldman-sachs-2016/what-if-i-told-you-gen-z-matters-more-than-millennials/903/; www.thoughtco.com/living-past-90-in-america-3321510; https://www.lindseypollak.com/different-generations-workplace-definitive-guide.

PERSPECTIVES ON POINT

Insights Gained from Personal Interviews by the Authors

JAVIER VELAZQUEZ, a DACA recipient, is the Founder and CEO of Uproot, an Atlanta-based company that helps small businesses plan and execute social media marketing campaigns. A strong believer in giving back, both financially and socially, he also is Co-founder of DiscoverHorizons, a Christian-based company offering outdoor gear and clothing. As he puts it, succinctly, "When you hire immigrants, you're essentially hiring entrepreneurs." From his point of view, immigrants generally arrive with an entrepreneurial focus, which is an essential part of their drive to make a new life for themselves. He also believes that it is crucial to demonstrate to politicians by using data on demographic changes over the last 25 to 50 years that it is this very influx of "go-getters" who are driving economic growth in the US.

RICHARD HOLDEN is Assistant Commissioner of Regional Operations in the San Francisco office of the US Department of Labor, a position that puts him in charge of data collection and information analysis for the Bureau of Labor Statistics in an office that represents an eight-state area. He points out that by 2026 all baby boomers will be over the age of 62, and will continue to constitute the largest age demographic in this country. Plus, while whites are still the majority of the population, they also form the segment that is experiencing the lowest population change. All other racial groups are changing at double-digit percentages, with the largest being Hispanics—who are also the youngest.

ELMY BERMEJO is the former West Coast Regional Representative for then-US Labor Secretary Tom Perez, having previously served as Director of Intergovernmental Affairs for the US Department of Labor. Having been involved in public policy issues for more than a quarter of a century, she has served on the staff of elected officials at both state and national levels. She remembers distinctly in the early 1980s a chief of staff in the US Senate office where she was helping with the hiring process, who said bluntly, "If you do not bring me a diverse group of candidates, you are not doing your job." When we ask her how she would recommend a recruiter in a small or medium-sized business could be convinced of that approach, she suggests what she calls a "Margaret Meade" approach. "Maybe the only Mexican that person has seen is someone who works in a neighbor's garden," she elaborates. "What about inviting her to coffee or a gathering? Let her sit next to a Latina who has a story that makes it clear they share some life experiences."

JOHN CLEVELAND is Senior Vice President, Human Resources, Internal Communications and Community Engagement at Seagate, the multi-billion-dollar company known for its hard drives, but self-described a bit more globally as "the essential connection between people and their content." The company was listed among Forbes' "Best Employers" in 2018, and with 50,000+ employed, that's no small feat. Cleveland is well aware of the prospects and pitfalls of various hiring practices. In an effort to encourage inclusion, Seagate has revised its application process to focus on skills, instead of college degree requirements for positions where that is feasible. He and his staff have discovered that candidates who may be interested in the opportunities may self select themselves out because they do not have the degree. He warns, too, that there needs to be a focus on diversity. A diverse team will lead to better decisions. And what about the board of directors in Corporate America? Cleveland has watched the process over time and notes that all too often policies and discussions about inclusion are reactive, and there is room for improvement in corporate America for more proactive analysis and action.

BART MYERS comes right to the point. In his profile for the website of Countable, the company he founded after Tivo acquired SideReel, another company he had founded, he is described as believing in the "brilliance of the Constitution, the need for compromise and a place for all sides to come together." [22] That same straightforward approach defines how he feels about inclusion and diversity. First, he goes deeper than the standard categories of gender, age, ethnicity. "When life experiences are different, so are points of view," he points out. "The rust belt is different from Berkeley, California." Second, he argues that inclusion/diversity must be part of the company "underlayment." Admitting that can be challenging, he turns to—not surprising—communication. "If the leaders don't make it absolutely clear that they see this as a core value, no one will recognize it."

MANNY RUIZ has launched and operated a series of successful ventures, but we are not sure he hasn't missed the best one. Reading his LinkedIn profile is more entertaining than watching Trevor Noah in top form (or Robin Williams, if he's your generation's comic master). We'll let you read it for yourself, but as a teaser—all direct quotes: (1) two-time high school senior; (2) TRYING to learn guitar for the FIFTH time; (3) subject of a national BestWestern TV ad. He's won awards for public relations, staged sell-out events, and is now in the business of providing entertainment based on nostalgia as experienced by various generations. The name of his company is

NostalgiaCon. The one before that was Hispanicize, and the focus was ethnic instead of generational. And why did he change? "I see the generational business as a growth industry. I realize your generation is out of tune with what my generation did.... Nostalgia, though, is universal." And it doesn't hurt that he wrote a diary when he was 13 years old, in the 1980s.

KINGSLEY ADVANI is a British investor who likes new: new ideas, new companies, new products, new investments, new opportunities of all sorts. He started investing in 2013, backing 50 companies and donating to nonprofits including: SENS Foundation, Methuselah Foundation, Stanford University, National University of Singapore. He is particularly interested in solving financial inclusion at scale and regenerative medicine to age-related disease. Advani's investments include Monzo, Robinhood, Abra, Coinbase, OncoSenX, Momentus, Demonpores, 64-x, and Nectome. His focus areas are financial inclusion, space propulsion, brain preservation and genome sequencing. Currently Founder and Partner at Chainfund Capital, he has worked with (a very partial list) Airbnb, Uber, and IBM. At this writing he lists on his LinkedIn page investments in companies that involve such elements as cryptocurrency, blockchain, water-powered propulsion for in-space transportation, launch systems for small satellites...you get the idea. He is bullish, to say the least, about the rise of Millennial investors, whom he characterizes as also liking what's new and edgy, partial to technology and ready to adopt early and often new ways of doing business, communicating, achieving. "We Millennials want what is transparent and good for the environment," he says, "and the more inclusive the decision-making is (and, of course, the potential client base) the more scalable." He sees a not-too-distant future in which the investment world will "include everyone, many, many $1k types."

STACEY FERREIRA knows a good bit about workforce management—tracking, scheduling, maximizing talent, communicating, employee engagement—the works. She is Co-founder and CEO of Forge, a talent-sharing platform, and the co-author of *2 Billion Under 20: How Millennials Are Breaking Down Age Barriers and Changing the World.* As that title suggests, she is bullish on how technology and humans are going to work together in the future. In her opinion, it will not be long before every company has a tech component, and humans in the workplace will be afforded more flexibility. She has specific advice for owners and managers who want to retain Millennial employees: "Don't be afraid to let them be free and flexible."

ALAINA PERCIVAL has never had a problem finding and filling leadership positions, so perhaps it is no surprise that she's developed a real passion for assuring that other talented women not only are able to do the same, but *know up front* that they can. As CEO and Board Chair of Women Who Code, a not-for-profit organization focused on inspiring women to excel in technology careers, she has taken the lead in developing a membership of more than 180,000 women in 98 countries worldwide. The organization currently offers more than 1,500 free technical and leadership events annually. "Women Who Code as I first knew it," she remembers, "was basically a small, powerful, helpful group, but more one that might be described as 'our little secret.' Yes, it's been a lot of hard work to get to this stage, but when you see the impact you can have that's a strong driver to continue."

Asked about what she and her team do to ensure their own hiring practices remain inclusive, she notes that they have a strong focus on avoiding choices that might actually become limiting.

To assume that someone's background must match the skill set we assign to a specific position is to miss others whose talents may not be limited to their previous education or experience. For that reason, we don't begin the hiring process by collecting resumes and identifying which applicants we wish to interview. Instead, we send applicants our "challenge" first. We then evaluate how they have responded. And still anything we think could create a bias—universities attended, even names if there's a chance they are friends of friends, etc.—has been blinded.

MARY PAPAZIAN has spent her career working in higher education, and as the current President of San Jose State University is the only female Armenian American university president in the country. In our interview she notes that people who spend their formative years and some of their free time as adults in small communities that are ethnically defined have an *advantage*, and it is one that few other people speaking to the topic of inclusion mention. "Most people quite naturally spend the majority of their time with others who share their socioeconomic identity, and thereby many of their interests," she begins. "But when you are a member of a small community where people with like national or ethnic backgrounds gather, you have the opportunity to interact with those whose professions, whose social or economic status, and whose intellectual interests may be quite different from your own."

From her current experience working with a student body that is strikingly diverse, she also has come to realize that we as Americans tend to label groups according to large geographic areas that encompass very different cultures. "Just over a third of our students are Asians or Pacific Islanders, but that most certainly does not signal homogeneity. Being Japanese is quite different from being Vietnamese. We spend a lot of time working on intentionality to assure that there is no 'invisible' population that we are somehow missing." Under Papazian's leadership, the university has also created an Office of Diversity, Equity and Inclusion, to make that intentionality a part of day-to-day operations.

KATHY WONG is the Chief Diversity Officer at San Jose State, and she adds a bit of a parable to explain the issues the university and organizations like it are dealing with.

> The octopus is one of the world's smartest invertebrates. As it moves across the ocean floor, it has the capacity to camouflage itself, but the distance from the brain to its tentacles is too great for an immediate adaptation, so it depends on its tentacles to sense and change to the immediate environment (Sagrin, 2012). That is similar to the situation that arises when the CEO, COO and board of directors understand a process or policy, but it is really important for the people on the ground to do the work. They need the autonomy to innovate. That's how creativity happens. The leadership simply cannot understand the needs or preferences of all groups.

KAREN CHUPKA has been on the staff of the Consumer Technology Association for 30 years, rising through the ranks as the organization grew and changed to match the industry it serves. She is very much aware that her story is quite different from the norm among those who work in technology, but cheerfully points out that "different" does not necessarily connote "disadvantaged." She insists, "Inclusion is not just about men and women, privileged and not privileged. I am the one who is different. I opted not to go to college. I began my career as a secretary. But I am also the one people turn to for problem-solving. That's my favorite activity, and I usually succeed." And then she adds, just as candidly, "Once I have learned how, though, I am not interested in doing it again. I'm definitely one and done, so it's important that any team include those who are *not* like me." And would she have found it easier if she had opted for a degree? She's thoughtful, but firm:

> Maybe, sometimes. With all of the possibilities that exist today and all of the talented and skilled people, it makes sense. It also makes sense that investors have lots of options, and they want to know that business leaders are skilled. But then it's also possible to have a pile of degrees, and no clue about how to start and/or run a business. When you know what your job is and how to do it, and are not afraid to express and opinion, your value becomes pretty obvious.

MEHAK VOHRA can speak with authority on the issues that arise when generations seek to work together. A member of the Gen Z complement, she notes that because of the stark differences between her generation and Millenials, it can be difficult for Gen Zers to be given the opportunity to make their own decisions. At the same time, she stresses the importance of listening to and learning from the experiences of others.

Founder of two companies that have been widely featured on the national media—OnDelta, focusing on training the next generation of marketers, and Jamocha Media, a marketing and personal branding firm—she notes that when she began her career she was counseled that her original concept was not scalable. "I took that to heart, asked myself how I could create a project that is scalable, and achieved success that would not have been possible otherwise," she explains. "I am a big believer in seeking out and listening to other people's descriptions of their experiences, so that I don't make those same mistakes myself."

ENDNOTES

1 Mark Milke, "Why Sears Failed: Lessons from Winston Churchill," www.theglobeandmail. com/report-on-business/rob-commentary/why-sears-failed-lessons-from-winston-churchill/ article36547603/.

2 Jonathan Vespa, David M. Armstrong, and Lauren Medina, "Demographic Turning Points for the United States: Population Estimates and Projections for 2020 to 2060," www.census.gov/ content/dam/Census/library/publications/2018/demo/P25_1144.pdf.

3 William H. Frey, "The US Will Become 'Minority White' in 2045, Census Projects: Youthful minorities of the engine of future growth," www.brookings.edu/blog/the-avenue/2018/03/14/ the-us-will-become-minority-white-in-2045-census-projects/.

4 Anthony Cilluffo and D'Vera Cohn, "7 Demographic Trends Shaping the US and the World in 2018," www.pewresearch.org/fact-tank/2018/04/25/7-demographic-trends-shaping-the-u-s-and-the-world-in-2018/.

5 www.theatlantic.com/sponsored/goldman-sachs-2016/what-if-i-told-you-gen-z-matters-more-than-millennials/903/.

6 John Wang, "Corporate America Still Lacks Leaders of Color and That's a Problem," www. huffpost.com/entry/corporate-america-still-lacks-leaders-of-color-and-thats-a-problem_n_5b d1f2eae4b0d38b58813fc2.

7 Pamela N. Danziger, "Global Consumer Trends for 2019 and the Brands that Are Out in Front of Them," www.forbes.com/sites/pamdanziger/2019/01/13/6-global-consumer-trends-and-brands-that-are-out-in-front-of-them-in-2019/#284d8f5b4fe4.

8 Courtney Buchanan, "How Millenials and Gen Z Are Reshaping the Future of Work: The Future Workforce Report," www.upwork.com/blog/2019/03/millennials-genz-future-workforce-report/.

9 "Towards a Reskilling Revolution: Industry-Led Action for the Future of Work, Centre for a New Economy and Society Insight Report," (Geneva, Switzerland: World Economic Forum in collaboration with Boston Consulting Group), www3.weforum.org/docs/WEF_Towards_a_ Reskilling_Revolution.pdf.

10 "Immigrant Founders of the 2017 Fortune 500," Center for American Entrepreneurship, http://startupsusa.org/fortune500/.

11 Ian Hathaway, "Almost Half of Fortune 500 Companies Were Founded by American Immigrants or Their Children," www.brookings.edu/blog/the-avenue/2017/12/04/almost-half-of-fortune-500-companies-were-founded-by-american-immigrants-or-their-children.

12 Niall McCarthy, "The Massive Wage Gap Between US Citizens and Immigrants," [Infographic], www.forbes.com/sites/niallmccarthy/2017/03/07/the-massive-wage-gap-between-u-s-citizens-and-immigrants-infographic/#1c511b013e65.

13 Antonio Flores, "How the US Hispanic Population Is Changing," www.pewresearch.org/fact-tank/2017/09/18/how-the-u-s-hispanic-population-is-changing/.

14 Parker Morse, "Six Facts About the Hispanic Market that May Surprise You," www.forbes. com/sites/forbesagencycouncil/2018/01/09/six-facts-about-the-hispanic-market-that-may-surprise-you/#2a2dcde85f30.

15 Michael A. Olguin, "6 Reasons Marketing to Hispanics Makes Sense," www.inc.com/michael-olguin/6-reasons-marketing-to-hispanics-makes-sense.html.

16 https://www.inc.com/michael-olguin/6-reasons-marketing-to-hispanics-makes-sense.html.

17 Sylvia Ann Hewlett, Noni Allwood, and Laura Sherbin, "US Latinos Feel They Can't Be Themselves at Work," https:hbr.org/2016/10/u-s-latinos-feel-they-cant-be-themselves-at-work.

18 Tasneem Afridi, "What It's Like to be a Muslim Woman at Work," www.refinery29.com/en-us/2017/09/172-485/muslim-woman-workplace-experience.

19 Alex Lindsey, Eden King, Ashley Membere, and Ho Kwan Cheung, "Two Types of Diversity Training that Really Work," https://hbr.org/2017/07/two-types-of-diversity-training-that-really-work.

20 Tal Eyal, Mary Steffel, and Nicholas Epley, "Research: Perspective-Taking Doesn't Help You Understand What Others Want," https://hbr.org/2018/10/research-perspective-taking-doesnt-help-you-understand-what-others-want.

21 Rachel Thomas, Marianne Cooper, PhD, Ellan Konar, PhD, Megan Rooney, Mary Noble-Tolla, PhD, Ali Bohrer, Lareina Ye, Alexis Krivkovich, Irina Starikova, Kelsey Robinson, Marie-Claude Hadeau, and Nicole Robinson, PhD, "Women in the Workplace 2018," (LeanIn and McKinsey and Co., 2018) https://womenintheworkplace.com/.

22 Emily Chang, "How Redfin Is Breaking Up the Boys' Club of Silicon Valley," www.fastcompany.com/90312451/how-redfin-is-breaking-up-the-boys-club-of-silicon-valley.

CHAPTER FIVE

Inclusion That Drives Innovation

—

In the late 1980s, speaking at a meeting of corporate CEOs all old enough to remember World War II, most of them American and most entrepreneurs, Nobel Scientist Luis Alvarez recalled his experience working at Los Alamos. (Alvarez and his son are also the scientists best known for their theory that the extinction of the dinosaurs followed a meteor impact.) He had been assigned to fly in a plane that followed the Enola Gay, and drop a receptacle in which he had folded a letter he had written to a Japanese scientist also involved in atomic research. The letter said, in essence, that the bomb the Enola Gay carried was not the only one. As Alvarez explained it, American military and political strategists were afraid that the Hiroshima bombing would not have the anticipated deterrent effect if the Japanese were to believe it could not be replicated. And a message from one scientist to another might be believed.

At the end of his presentation, Alvarez held up the letter. Not only had it reached its addressee; it had been returned. The room was quiet. The amount of trust that obviously existed between writer and recipient had clearly "leveled a playing field" with global effect. This and stories like it may well have helped create what has become an active scholarly investigation of the effect of cross-cultural collaboration, played out in the American business community by immigrants' very significant contributions on the innovation front.

Reporting on just one such study, Simon Constable, author of *The WSJ Guide to the 50 Economic Indicators that Really Matter*, began his February 2019 post on forbes.com[1] with this sentence: "Most people won't like this." The "this" to which he refers is a report generated by a US Census Bureau researcher in collaboration with a team from George Mason University. Seeking to measure just how much immigrants contribute to innovation, the group studied 7,400 firms with 11,000 owners. They found that overall immigrants handily outperformed their native-born counterparts in technology innovation. Aware that immigrants, in general, are better educated, they controlled for that variable, and the immigrant advantage held.

> How do we advise people to make companies fit for the candidates instead of vice versa?
>
> ~ Rebeca Hwang | General Partner & Co-founder, Rivet Ventures

There continue to be multiple studies that measure innovation in terms of patent production. One 2018 project based at Stanford University and carried out in collaboration with the National Bureau of Economic Research (NBER)[2] produced these findings (among others):

- The contribution of high-skilled immigrants to innovation persists also when the measures include patent citations, the economic value of patents and product reallocation.
- When the immigrants work on teams, the teams are more likely to rely on foreign technology, to collaborate

with foreign inventors, and to have their work cited in foreign markets.

- In the group studied, 16 percent were tagged as immigrants, and they were responsible for 30 percent of US aggregate innovation, with data used beginning in 1976.
- Immigrants account for 26 percent of US-based Nobel prize winners between 1990 and 2000.

There are interesting qualitative findings, too. The researchers suggest that:

- The high-skilled immigrants disproportionately choose to live in highly productive counties.
- In some work environments, they are isolated and thereby not able to participate in teams to the degree that they might—with measurable positive results.
- When teams do incorporate immigrants, if the team leader dies before the project is completed, that death lowers productivity from 28 percent to 50 percent if the leader were American; 50 percent to 60 percent if s/he were a skilled immigrant.

It is important to remember, of course, that the NBER study focused on the highly skilled segment of foreigners coming to the US. It is easy to believe that were the skills to encompass a full range of employees, the results might differ. Still, by definition, the Americans working on product and process innovation can be expected to be highly skilled as well, so if oranges are going to accompany the apples on one side, they should on the other.

NOTHING NEW UNDER THE SUM (typo-intended)

Another NBER study that has been a darling of economists and social scientists alike focuses on the effect immigrants have had on innovation beginning in the late 19th century.[3] Researchers Ufuk Akcigit and John Grigsby from the University of Chicago and Tom Nicholas from the Harvard Business School, found:

- Between 1880 and 1940, immigrants accounted for 19.6 percent of US inventors. Today, that's about 30 percent.
- From 1940 to 2000, sectors with more foreign-born inventors produced more patents.
- Despite being more productive, immigrants were paid less on average than their domestic counterparts, as were female and black inventors.

ANECDOTES ABOUND— INVENTIONS AND IDEATIONS

"Aw, c'mon," you're thinking. "What exactly is ideation?" Here, at least, it's an idea that grew to create a transition. The point is, not all innovation involves inventing something. Sometimes significant transformation happens when a tuned-in type sees something that others fail to see. And immigrants are doing quite well, thank you very much, on both fronts. Moving more or less chronologically:

- Alexander Graham Bell, Scotland, like you don't already know.

- John Nordstrom, Sweden, opened a shoe store with a partner in 1901. Nordstrom revenue for the 12 months ending January 31, 2019, was $15.860 billion.
- Albert Einstein, Germany, uh huh.
- Leo Sziland, Hungary, helped persuade the US to work on the atomic bomb; encouraged Einstein to warn Roosevelt on the potential outcome.
- Ebay Founder Pierre Omidyar, born in Paris to Iranian parents, saw that collectors needed a way to connect and trade.
- Comcast Founder Daniel Aaron, Germany, worked as a journalist and turned what he learned working on a story about a cable company into a top-notch competitor in the industry.
- When Jerry Yang, Taiwan, and his American partner, David Filo, first formed their company it was called "David and Jerry's Guide to the World Wide Web." Now Yahoo (for Yet Another Hierarchical Officious Oracle) and now owned by Verizon, it elevated the two to multiple lists of "the richest."
- Hubert Joly, CEO of Best Buy, was named one of the "Best CEOs in World" by *CEOWorld* magazine in 2018. He was born in France. The year after he took over at Best Buy, the company's stock tripled.

It is particularly interesting to note that a number of the companies the average US citizen might well describe as the "most American" were founded by immigrants. Included are the likes of Procter and Gamble, DuPont, Colgate-Palmolive, Kraft, Honeywell...the list goes on. If it is expanded to include those born in America of immigrant parents, the numbers and names multiply several times over. The story of one of that group provides an excellent example of how ingenuity, focus and courage can win the day.

Amadeo Petro Gianninni was born in San Mateo, California. His father was originally drawn to the U.S. from Italy by the 1849 California Gold Rush. Twenty years later the elder Gianninni returned to Italy and married Amadeo's mother. They bought a farm and began to sell fruits and vegetables. Amadeo began his career as a produce dealer, but after marrying the daughter of a real estate magnate, retired early to administer his father-in-law's estate. When he gained a seat on the board of a savings and loan his father owned, he saw a chance to provide banking services for the immigrant community, which at that time had no access to banks. When the rest of the board could not be persuaded to work with him, he quit and formed his own bank, the Bank of Italy. This was 1904. Two years later when the San Francisco earthquake devastated the city, he used a garbage wagon to take the money from his vault to his home in San Mateo, out of the fire zone. For weeks, he was one of very few bankers who could honor withdrawal requests and make loans.

A believer in branch banking, Gianninni expanded the Bank of Italy throughout California and put the banks in a holding company—a relatively new concept for banking at that time—known as Transamerica. Eventually the bank was merged with and became called the Bank of America. The only banker named to the *Time* 100 for the 20th century, Gianninni is considered to be the inventor of many modern banking practices. And his influence does not stop with banking. While he was at the helm, his bank loaned Walt Disney the money to make *Snow White* and provided financial backing for William Hewlett and David Packard, to name just a couple more.[4]

A GENERATIVE NEXUS

As important as the contribution of individual immigrants has been and continues to be, the effect inclusion has on the work of teams is not only important, according to some analysts, but crucial. In an article published by *Scientific American* in 2014,[5] Katherine W. Phillips argues that the widely accepted notion that inclusive groups are more innovative than homogeneous ones because their experiences and skill vary is only part of the story. Not only is there a richer trove of information, she contends, but people who interact with others who are different are forced to prepare better, to be ready to understand and incorporate alternative viewpoints, and to realize that the path to consensus will require more effort. Phillips knows of what she writes. She is currently the Reuben Mark Professor of Organizational Character and Director of the Sanford C. Bernstein & Co. Center for Leadership and Ethics at Columbia Business School, and before that was on the faculty at Northwestern University's Kellogg School where she was founding Co-director of the Center on Science of Diversity.

Here are some of the findings she cites:
- In a study of the management teams of the S&P Composite 1500 firms from 1992 through 2006, business professors Cristian Deszö of the University of Maryland and David Ross of Columbia University wrote that they found "female representation in top management leads to an increase of $42 million in firm value."
- Professors at the University of Texas at Dallas surveyed executives at 177 national banks and found that when bank presidents emphasized innovation, increases in racial diversity were related to enhanced financial performance.

- When a team at Credit Suisse Research Institute examined 2,360 companies worldwide from 2005 to 2011, they found those with one or more women on their boards produced higher average returns on equity, lower net debt to equity and better average growth.

Pat Gelsinger, CEO of VMware, reports that his company has a policy that requires that "all final interview slates must include at least one female or Under Represented Minority (URM)."

Another comprehensive study of the connection between inclusion and innovation was conducted by the Boston Consulting Group and the Technical University of Munich in 2016 and focused on 171 German, Swiss and Austrian countries.[6] The definitions on which the research is based are telling. To measure inclusion (which they call diversity), the researchers considered not only age, gender, and country of origin, but also what percentage of managers had worked at other companies and how their academic training differed. Innovation revenue was defined as the share of revenues generated by new products and services in the most recent three-year period.

The authors write that "diversity and innovation don't affect each other directly, the way sales of umbrellas by a street vendor rise on a rainy day," but instead the relationship is more complex. Still the two "move together" in statistically significant ways, which means that companies with higher levels of diversity—we would say "inclusion"—get more revenue from new products and services. The effect also is greater at companies with multiple product lines, and increases with the size of the company.

PERSPECTIVES ON POINT

Insights Gained from Personal Interviews by the Authors

ANKA WITTENBERG spent five years as Chief Diversion and Inclusion Officer at SAP SE and has since 2011 served as Senior Vice President for Global Human Resources at SAP AG. She is dedicated to, focused on and all about being accountable for driving innovation with a commitment to inclusion. It bears remembering that SAP was the first US tech company to receive EDGE (Global Economic Dividends for Gender Equality) gender certification. And gender isn't the only focus. In 2013, SAP began an "Autism at Work" program, which now includes more than 140 employees in 12 countries. Wittenberg is also Chair of the Board of Directors of the World Childhood Foundation, headquartered in her native Germany. In addition to the power of inclusive practices to improve corporate financial performance and market penetration, which she refers to as "company momentum," Wittenberg sees a "free-flowing culture with diverse perspectives and ideas" as being directly responsible for increased collaboration and creativity. As she puts it: "When process meets culture, awareness, diversity and technology, real solutions can be found." Not surprisingly, for SAP those solutions include making products and services accessible for customers—and potential customers.

TIM HWANG, a Korean-American, founded FiscalNote in 2013, as a state legislative tracking service. He was completing his undergraduate degree at Princeton University, and put together the new company with two high school friends. Now one of the largest tech employers headquartered in the Washington, DC, area, FiscalNote includes among its clients influential law firms, legal departments and governments worldwide and has been named a World Economic Forum Technology Pioneer. Hwang speaks directly to both the importance of inclusion and its complexity. He recognizes that CEOs who argue that lack of inclusion stems largely from a "pipeline problem" are often criticized, but insists that the problem does, indeed, exist. "Go to a computer science classroom at, say, MIT or Stanford," he suggests. "Sit at the back, and take a look at how many females there are, or for that matter, members of the underrepresented classes." That he maintains is one of the reasons for the problem, but not an excuse. "You have to go where you find what you're looking for," he says. "We go to places such as Wellesley and Smith." Another issue he recognizes, especially in terms of capturing the innovative power of inclusion, is the need for mentors. Bottom line, Hwang considers the US population to be one of the most diverse in the world, but recognizes that even so, committed leadership is required to link inclusion and innovation successfully.

RODRIGO GARZA, CEO of Miami-based Flexinvest, an investment platform that offers a door to the investment world for new and experienced investors, makes no bones about what he thinks it takes to build a business, and for that matter a life. Born in Mexico, he came from a family culture that stressed education and travel, a combination that he believes creates a fertile ground for ambition and achievement. Having come to the US to "get the best education possible," he earned his Bachelor's Degree at the University of Pennsylvania, then added a Master's in Public Administration from the Kennedy School at Harvard, and an MBA with emphasis on entrepreneurship and innovation at the Sloan School of Management at MIT *simultaneously*. He is direct and emphatic when he discusses the value of encouraging the mixture of different points of view and different experiences. "That's how teams become more dynamic, thereby creating value for the customer and the company, ultimately leading to nothing but financial gains."

ALVARO SILBERSTEIN may take things sitting down, quite literally, because he has been wheelchair-bound since he was injured in an accident at the age of 18. But, as the English idiom suggests, he doesn't "take things lying down." In other words, his approach to a problem is to fight instead of fold, or perhaps better even, to find out. So it is that he and his friend Camilo Navarro, both of them from Chile, founded a company they call "Wheel the World," to offer the ultimate in inclusion to those with disabilities—the opportunity to visit some of what have been the world's most beautiful but inaccessible places. In December 2018 their company made headlines when it offered a trip to Peru's iconic Machu Picchu, only one of a number of trips planned for Latin America. That means navigating 300+ near vertical steps. It all began with Silberstein's using crowdfunding to sponsor the two men's own trip to a national park in Patagonia. Unabashed in his enthusiasm about how important mentoring has been in his life and business, Silberstein tells us: "I have had many mentors who have trusted in me on what we were doing when we had very little, and the type of recommendations that they give you make you feel confident and proud. It does not matter how small it is."

SWATI MYLAVARAPU basically swept the field when she grad-uated from Harvard University: Phi Beta Kappa, Truman Scholar, John Harvard Scholar, President of the International

Relations Council. Then, no surprise, she was a Rhodes Scholar. Her professional career (so far) has included positions at Quid, Square, and Kleiner Perkins Caulfield and Byers. She is Co-founder of The Arena, an organization devoted to making democracy accessible for newcomers and building the next generation of civic leaders, and Managing Partner of Incite.org, a San Francisco-based operation that is part investment fund and part foundation. Among the firms Incite has invested in is Nima, a company that provides tools for peo-ple suffering with allergies. "Not only was our team assigned to that project inclusionary in terms of gender, ethnicity, age, etc.," she said. "We made sure it included people with food allergies themselves."

Whatever the specific situation, Mylavarapu believes teams are stronger when they incorporate a collection of different ideas and experiences. "Like everyone else, entrepreneurs like investors who have had life experiences similar to theirs."

TINA SEELIG has a somewhat unusual title: Professor of the Practice, Management Science and Engineering at Stanford University. But then, it would be difficult to come up with a title that describes what she does. Note that word "does." She is involved in a good bit more "doing" than in "professing." Let's "do" the list:

- Having earned a PhD in Neuroscience from the Stanford University School of Medicine, she has since garnered six prestigious awards for her acumen in education and innovation.
- She has written 17 books and educational games. *Scientific American* published her two books on the chemistry of cooking; Chronicle Books produced her 12 "Games for Your Brain" targeted to children; and HarperCollins published her books focused on creativity and putting ideas to work.

We particularly like the title of the latest one: *Creativity Rules: Get Ideas Out of Your Head and Into the World.*

- The courses she teaches deal with creativity, innovation and entrepreneurship, and outside the classroom she addresses those same issues, plus team-building and risk-taking, with blog posts, podcasts, TED Talks, online courses, media interviews, etc.

- In short, she is as creative in her choice of communication channels as she is adept at communicating creativity.

In our interview, Seelig traces how the interplay between inclusion or the lack of it can be dealt with by a combination of courage and imagination. "It's important to speak up," she explains. "Give yourself a challenge. Say just one thing. Even if it doesn't work out the way you had hoped, you make yourself easy to help."

To Seelig, the link between creativity and entrepreneurship is obvious, and an environment rich in different approaches jump-starts creativity. As she writes in her book, *inGenius: A Crash Course in Creativity:*

> Very innovative companies, such a Twitter, know how important this type of cross-pollination is to creativity in their businesses, and they make an effort to hire people with unusual skills, knowing that diversity of thinking will certainly influence the development of their products.[7]

STEVE BENNETT has the kind of leadership experience that is increasingly rare: it includes decades-long experience in the world that would not typically be defined as being limited to "tech," (much of it with GE), and multiple CEO positions with companies that are globally known within the tech industry. One of those was Intuit, where he served as CEO from 2000 to 2008. On the subject of innovation, he says, "Inclusion is important for not only innovation but better decision-making." He believes an idea comes from a single individual working within an environment that fosters the creation of ideas, and grows to fruition when there is an established process to nurture it. He explains:

> Our best success at Intuit was when we started with a cross-functional team, instituted Intuit Founder Scott Cook's process called 'Follow Me Home" by sending them to actually observe customers—just observe, not ask questions—and had them develop a product idea, or you might say focus on 'proof of concept,' based on what they had learned. That's how we added the payment function of Quickbooks. It was a small cross-functional team led by a woman who I believe may now be in a senior role at Google. They saw customers in retail settings taking the receipts and entering the numbers, so they designed a point of sale product. It actually is quite similar to what Scott used to call the 'unexpected surprise.' You may remember that his idea for Quickbooks was born when he watched his wife balancing her checkbook sitting at the kitchen table.

TIM DRAPER is Headmaster of Draper University and Founding Partner of Draper Associates. His perspective on innovation is simple, explicit and compelling:

> Innovation comes from everywhere. Anyone willing to work hard on a project can come up with new thoughts and ideas for how to improve, automate, enhance, speed up, make less costly our current way of doing things. While I never explicitly force inclusion in my companies, the best ones naturally include the best people for the job, and those best people come from everywhere.

COURTNEY VANLONKHUYZEN WELTON cred-
its her work in an Asian environment, a part of her assignment as
General Counsel with Lenovo Mobile Business Group, with creating a "re-appreciation of the art of relationship." Now serving
as Senior Vice President, Chief Ethics and Compliance Officer,
Chief Privacy Officer, and Deputy General Counsel for Innovation
Law at Allstate, she candidly admits that her natural bent when
assuming a new position is "to jump in and fix things." Instead, in
this case, she realized that the most effective initial strategy was
what she terms a "listening tour," designed not only to inform her
own decision-making, but also to build an environment wherein the
ideas she came up with "would be listened to." She also points out
that it is a natural behavior no matter what one's profession—"even
psychologists do it"—to "forget that other people don't live in
our world." So, when presenting an idea to say, financial professionals, she talks about "cost models." For sales and marketing
staffers the same idea might be described in terms of benefits and
how to communicate them. And determining the best approach,
of course, means defining inclusion as a lens not focused merely
on groups identified by such labels as gender, age, ethnicity, gender preference, etc., but also life experiences that give birth to
preferences—those who live alone, those who run marathons, etc.
"A broader lens guards against blind spots," she concludes. "At
Allstate, our present and potential customers are everyone. Our
business is protecting people from life's uncertainties." Named for
the 5th time by Ethisphere as one of the world's most ethical companies, this is a business in good hands.

MARTHA-EDITH HERNANDEZ has made it her busi-
ness—literally—to know about innovation, with particular attention
to how it can be affected by cultural ideas. Called "Startup Life
Coach LLC," that business builds on her experience running the
National Science Foundation Innovation Corps—Lean LaunchPad

course at UC Berkeley, during which she trained hundreds of startup founders in Tunisia, Mexico and Uruguay. Having moved from the San Francisco Bay area to Omaha, Nebraska, she has now discovered that cultural differences can be just as potent from region to region within one country as they can from country to country. "Silicon Valley calls itself the 'Innovation Capital of the World,' and its leaders are sure they are aware of most of the problems contemporary society faces. That's incorrect," she argues. "It's an incestuous, if I may use that word, pool of ideas. No one is ready to step out of her or his comfort zone. How many investors understand the world of agriculture or are ready to listen to the ideas of the people who operate in it? Yet the work ethic in the Midwest is beyond the imagination of much of the Western population." Also recruited by Singularity to provide mentorship on a pro bono basis and still involved with the Tunisia chapter of the Founder Institute, Hernandez centers her coaching/mentoring around a core theory that attitude, as in a growth mentality, is central to any successful business strategy, and that such an attitude is home-grown.

YAI VARGAS has been working on issues of inclusion since 2006. First in corporate settings and now with consulting practices of her own: The Latinista, offering skill-building, career advancement workshops for women, and Yai Vargas Diversity Consulting, through which she offers a full array of services. Her work with Employee Resource Groups has been particularly extensive, and she stresses how important it is to direct those groups into innovative programs. "ERGs work best," she says, "when they focus on two things: (1) making a difference in the community; and (2) creating innovative programs that have a measurable effect on the bottom line." She adds that she advises these groups, whatever their shared experience, be it ethnic, gender, or anything else, to avoid the "three Fs": food, flags and fun. "You have a Cinco de Mayo party, and the CEO comes to find out how your line item in the budget is being spent. Hmmm, how are you doing?" There are multiple case studies of ERGs who have, instead, used their knowledge of the group they represent to create a new product, source it, brand it, write the mission statement, develop the slogan—in essence, capitalize on the fact that they don't just know their segment of the market, they *are* that segment. Vargas encourages ERGs as well as individuals navigating their way to career advancement to focus on what is "strategic, accessible and measurable."

DANIELA ARRUDA, Co-founder of San Francisco-based BABEL Ventures, sees the value of creative thinking in the work that she does as well as in the work of companies she and her colleagues fund. "One of my largest regrets in investing in startups," she says, "is to have failed to invest in some, by using a rigorous technical evaluation rather than intuition." And, she adds, finding the best potential investments is driven by access, which in turn derives from relationships. "Before we created the Fund, we worked long hours creating relationships so we could have access to the best deals and to the investors who would come with us on this journey."

MACI PETERSON PHILITAS has a view on inclusion and innovation that is less about how one affects the other than it is about how an individual can be affected by one or both, with the result being how much the individual is able to learn to take charge of her/his situation. On the topic of inclusion, Philitas' recent move to Morocco has been a revelation. "In the US," she explains, "we insist it is so easy to speak our language, to participate in our economy, but in the end that's not realistic. Here in Morocco, I have come to see what it is really like to be welcomed. In one instance, I'm still learning the language here and I was at the government office to sign a document. When I faced a language problem, the man I was dealing with left his office and went out into the hall to try to find someone who could speak English. This is a culture where relationships are based on community and family. In Morocco, people seem pre-disposed to say 'yes' whereas at home in the US, it often seems people are trying to look for the quickest way to say 'No.' "

And "No" was the answer Peterson received when she asked if there were a way to recall sent email messages. Her reaction? Build one! When she pitched her idea at SXSW (the Austin-based conference on what's coming in film, culture, music and technology), she won first prize. Convinced she was onto something, she contacted a friend she had met at another conference while she was in college, and together they founded On Second Thought, first providing an app and then moving to an API solution.

KEVIN WASHINGTON is national CEO of the YMCA, and his view of inclusion offers an element that none of the other 130+ individuals we interviewed for this book mentioned. "You know when you walk into a room that you are in some way 'different.' Before you do anything else, you need to look into a mirror and be content with the person that you see." In other words, inclusion begins at home. Once that's accomplished, Washington has a very defined list of what your potential employer needs to do to complete the picture. The six steps he has put into place and considers crucial are:

1. Designate a staff position that has responsibility for inclusion and make it be a direct report to the CEO.
2. Make your leadership team be representative of the teams you want throughout the organization.
3. Recruit a board that will be representative as well, starting with skill sets and incorporating inclusivity.

4. Select partnerships, vendors, etc. on shared values of inclusivity.
5. Educate the communities in which you work on your policies, practices and procedures.
6. Create within your workplace and your community a safe place for all...ALL people.

ENDNOTES

1   Simon Constable, "The Most Innovative US Tech Entrepreneurs Aren't American, They're Foreign-Born, a New Study Shows," https://www.forbes.com/sites/simonconstable/2019/02/27/the-most-innovative-u-s-tech-entrepreneurs-are-foreign/#4ad1340d2736.

2   Shai Bernstein, Rebecca Diamond, Timothy McQuade and Beatriz Pousada, "The Contribution of High-Skilled Immigrants to Innovation in the United States," https://web.stanford.edu/~diamondr/bdmp_oct2018.pdf.

3   Ufuk Akcigit, John Grigsby and Tom Nicholas, "Immigration and the Rise of American Ingenuity," https://static1.squarespace.com/static/57fa873e8419c230ca01eb5f/t/5897feaaa5790a1076552f55/1486356139676/w23137.pdf.

4   https://www.pbs.org/wgbh/theymadeamerica/whomade/giannini_hi.html.

5   Katherine W. Phillips, "How Diversity Makes Us Smarter: Being around people who are different from us makes us more creative, more diligent and harder-working," https://www.scientificamerican.com/article/how-diversity-makes-us-smarter/.

6   Roćio Lorenzo, Nicole Voigt, Karin Schetelig, Annika Zawadzki, Isabell Welpe, and Prisca Brosi, "The Mix That Mattters: Innovation Through Diversity," (Boston Consulting Group and Technical University of Munich, 2016) http://media-publications.bcg.com/22feb2017-mix-that-matters.pdf.

7   Seelig, Tina. inGenius: A Crash Course in Creativity.

CHAPTER SIX

Pipelines and How to Make Them Better

—

Despite a growing recognition among corporate leaders that inclusion and diversity are proven elements for stability and growth in the 21st century, many also admit that they are failing to meet their own expectations, not to mention projections. Often the plaint is a variation on: "We would really like to move faster, but there just are not enough qualified people in the pipeline."

If that is accurate, the first place to look, of course, is the pipeline itself. Techniques abound, and include:

Blinding: Removing from applications and resumes any information that can result in bias—conscious or not—is by no means a new process. Many believe it is actually derived from the symphony orchestra world, where for some time now musicians applying for a seat have been asked to perform behind a screen, because it became apparent that there was gender bias at work when evaluators could see the performers, given the small number of females in many orchestras.

- Different companies use different techniques, of course, but human resources professionals often suggest considering at least the following:
- Name: A National Bureau of Economic Research study[1] found that job applicants with "white" names had to send an average of 10 resumes to get a call back. For those with "African-American" names, the number was 15. Similarly, a Canadian study[2] found that those with Chinese, Indian

or Pakistani-sounding names were 28 percent less likely to land an interview than those with the same qualifications, but with English names. Obviously names also signal gender.

- Dates of birth or graduation: In a 2017 Federal Reserve Bank of San Francisco study,[3] 40,000 applications were sent out for 13,000 low-skill positions in 12 cities. Older "applicants," especially female ones, netted fewer interviews, in some fields as much as 47 percent fewer.
- Address: ZIP codes signal socioeconomic status, multifamily housing, etc.
- College/University Name: Again, some schools signal prestige, a certain base level of family income, etc.

AI evaluation programs: For many Americans old enough to remember pre-Internet news, Reuters is to newswire reporting what Campbell's is to canned soup. Around forever, trustworthy, it was something of a paradigm for branding, but in more recent years subject to challenge from competitors that use different marketing and distribution methods. It is more than a little ironic, therefore, that Reuters was the first to report in October 2018[4] that Amazon's team of machine-learning specialists had discovered a bug in their recruiting program. In setting the artificial intelligence (AI) program to evaluate resumes on a five-star system based on patterns in resumes Amazon had received during the past decade, they perpetuated a gender-bias. Most of those resumes had come from men, and as a result the AI program taught itself to remove resumes carrying certain terms, such as "women's," even to the point of downgrading resumes from graduates of two all-women's colleges.

Amazon disbanded the team, explaining those results were not the only source of rankings. Still, using AI remains problematic.

The Reuters report quotes results from a 2017 survey by CareerBuilder that indicated 55 percent of human resources managers anticipated that AI would be part of their work within five years. In January 2019, Glassdoor ran a post[5] describing the AI tools companies were using—specifically citing AllyO, TextRecruit and Montage—and the hiring processes of major companies, including AT&T, Allstate, Capital One, Five Guys, Hilton, Humana, Procter & Gamble, and ThredUp. Interviewees' comments were full of positive reactions to the efficiency and timeliness of the process. HR professionals suggest it actually improves access.

So, it would seem that those eager to fill the recruiting pipeline with a stream of candidates as diverse as it is skilled and experienced have the opportunity to do so. Still, there remain significant cautions.

Kartik Hosanagar, in his 2019 book *How Algorithms Are Shaping Our Lives and How We Can Stay in Control: A Human's Guide to Machine Intelligence*,[6] describes a 2015 Carnegie-Mellon study in which the researchers created 1,000 simulated user profiles, half male and half female. They had all 1,000 visit the top 100 employment websites, using Google. Interestingly, the Google algorithm showed the male profiles significantly more ads relating to high-paying positions than it did the female ones. There are multiple theories about the cause—including simply that women do not click on ads as frequently as men—but Hosanager points out that this raises concerns about "steering," a term and concept usually defined in terms of illegally guiding minority groups toward credit cards that are less advantageous. While it may be unintentional, he argues, it is certainly undesirable.

Because technology, specifically algorithms, will most probably continue to grow in use, not only in large-scale enterprises, where the size of the budget can encompass funds for development, but also within small and medium-sized corporations that can use the various firms and apps now on the market, it is crucial to take steps to identify bias early and eradicate it efficiently. The first of those steps, of course, is to admit that such bias is not only possible, but perhaps probable.

Careful use of language: Whether the first level of screening is accomplished by AI or by traditional methods, some companies unconsciously limit the number of applicants by the use of words that to some groups have a negative connotation. As Stanford University Professor Margaret Neale, whose research focuses largely on negotiation and team performance, suggests: "When you are doing recruiting, what does your recruiting say? The wording that you are using in your advertisement in itself stops some people from applying."

> Millennials care a lot about
> a democratic workplace,
> and they will vote with their feet.
>
> ~ David Hornik | Venture Capitalist

Training managers, hirers and interviewers: Bias is, of course, often unrecognized, and even unconscious. The Implicit Association Tests developed by Project Implicit have been used successfully by survey firms, including Pew Research,[7] but have also been criticized by various reporters and reviewers. You and your human resources colleagues can, of course, make your own judgments. The tests are found online at https://implicit.harvard.edu/implicit/.

Whatever techniques you choose to limit bias, it could be argued that one of your strongest approaches is to ensure that the team of individuals involved in the hiring process is itself inclusive. What's more, it is important that in creating an inclusive team you have avoided not only actual but apparent tokenism. How would a prospective employee in her 50s react if all of her interviewers were in their 20s and 30s? Or a team of eight, seven of whom fit that description?

> It's an error to use one interview
> process for all applicants,
> no matter what that process is.
>
> ~ Laszlo Bock | Author of *Work Rules*

Are your interviewers informed about the legal limitations on questions that can be asked in interviews? (See page page 106.) Many questions that seem quite innocent could be considered to be roundabout ways to find out about ethnicity, religious affiliation, age, gender and gender identity, political affiliation, etc. If there is information relevant to skills, specific job requirements or your corporate culture that would necessitate questions that might be interpreted as breaking one of these restrictions, how are the interviewers planning to get the information but remain not only legal but unbiased?

Jenny Dearborn, former Executive Vice President, Human Resources at SAP argues that it is crucial for all executives all the time to be talent ambassadors. "If you're in a leadership position, it's your all-the-time second job," she believes. What steps do you take or should you take to make that part of your culture?

Finally, it is important to remember that an interview constitutes a setting for two-way evaluation. Describing her decision to join Alsop Louie Partners, Ernestine Fu remembers: "What I cared about most was the people who work there."

ILLEGAL JOB INTERVIEW QUESTIONS

This information is collected from multiple sources, and does not constitute legal advice.

When were you born? When did you graduate from high school? When do you expect to retire?

Are you a native English speaker?

Where are you from originally?

What country are your parents from?

Do you own or rent your home? Whom do you live with and how are you related to her/him?

Are you dating anyone right now? Are you married or planning to get married?

Do you have or are you going to have children? If so, what will your child care arrangements be?

Will you be available to work on weekends or at night?

What holidays do you celebrate?

Do you go to church?

Have you ever been arrested? (Questions about conviction record may be ok in certain circumstances.)

How often do you call in sick? Do you have any disabilities?

Have you ever been addicted to drugs? (It is okay to ask about current drug usage, but not addiction. Asking about prior drug usage is deemed illegal in some instances.)

Do you have a bank account? Have you ever been declared bankrupt?

If you served in the military, what kind of discharge did you receive?

How do you feel about unions?

Will you take a lie detector test? (Some exceptions apply, such as government, pharmaceutical and security firms.)

I see you're in the National Guard. Do you expect to deploy soon?

For Additional Information, check: www.cheatsheet.com/money-career/illegal-job-interview-questions-you-dont-have-to-answer.html/ and www.betterteam.com/illegal-interview-questions

Today women constitute at least 49 percent in many computer science programs. That's up from 13–18 percent, and by all accounts on the skill front these women are equal to or better than their male counterparts.

~ Eric Schmidt | former CEO of Google

Creating and exhibiting a corporate culture that is welcoming to applicants with desired skills and experience: Perhaps one of the most comprehensive studies that addresses this issue, in this case having to do with gender bias, is the 2018 LeanIn and McKinsey&Co report entitled *Women in the Workplace.*[8] Some of the statistical findings of the report are telling:

- Women account for 48 percent of the corporate pipeline for entry-level positions, 38 percent of managerial positions overall and only 23 percent of the C-suite level.
- Even though gender diversity should be a business priority, only 38 percent of companies set targets for gender representation, 12 percent inform their employees on gender metrics, and 42 percent hold senior leaders accountable for making progress in this area.
- Employees are not sold! About half see gender diversity as a corporate priority where they work, and two in ten think it's basically lip service.
- Microaggressions in the workplace affect 64 percent of women and 71 percent of lesbian women. Outright sexual harassment has faced more than one in three at some point in their careers.

- And are companies doing anything to address these issues and make their culture not merely inclusive, but also respectful? Employees don't think so. Biased language and behavior is challenged in only 27 percent of the cases; disrespectful behavior 40 percent; and claims of harassment 32 percent.
- Women who are the "only" in a specific workplace setting (that's one in five) are 1.5 times more likely to think of leaving.

The formula the report suggests is straightforward:

1. Track representation by gender, race, gender and race, then set targets and share these metrics with employees and hold senior leaders, managers and directors responsible.
2. Make hiring and promotions fair by again setting targets, using automated resume screening tools [*that have been vetted for hidden bias*], setting clear criteria before the process begins, requiring diverse slates of candidates, assuring that all interviewers have been trained to anticipate and avoid unconscious bias, and once the process is complete checking again for bias.
3. Assure that senior leaders and managers not only agree with but champion inclusion and diversity.
4. Do what is necessary to build a respectful culture.
5. Limit the "only" experience.
6. Take a flexible approach to give employees the ability to comfortably balance work and family life.

Obviously, these strategies could easily be redirected to other groups as well. The tactics might vary, but the intent is very much the same. As are the results, since an employee who witnesses another employee being treated respectfully expects the same treatment. As Goethe famously said:

"The way you see people is the way you treat them, and the way you treat them is the way they become."

~ Johann Wolfgang Von Goethe

PERSPECTIVES ON POINT

Insights Gained from Personal Interviews by the Authors

SALLY PERA spent 13 years as the CEO of the Association for Corporate Growth, Silicon Valley, and retired in 2018. She remembers vividly the change that took place in her own organization when a financial services firm based in Germany opened an office in Silicon Valley and one of the executives joined the board. "It is important," she maintains, "to go out and find people who grew up in different countries, have had different experiences, are at different points in life, and most of all have different ways of thinking." She admits, though, that doing so effectively may take some sort of political mandate, similar to those some European countries have adopted. "To take the big mind," she says, "takes a big commitment."

TENZIN SELDON knows whereof she speaks. As a Tibetan refugee who spent her childhood in the Indian Himalayas, she has witnessed more than a few of the challenges that arise for immigrants. The organization she founded is known as Kinstep, and it is a business-to-business platform designed to help immigrants who have been pre-qualified find employment by matching them directly with opportunities within a given community. At the same time, the group works against the all-too-common "under-the-table" practices that lead to exploitation.

Seldon is firm about what she sees as the major problems in recruiting and hiring. Insisting that it is all but impossible to create an inclusive corporate culture unless the senior management team is itself representative of that value, she also notes that those who complain about the "pipeline" are failing to create an environment for talented immigrants who might otherwise apply. "These are not people who are comfortable with the Silicon Valley style of interview—a blackboard, a team of people asking questions, etc. And the real point is that if the management team included people with similar backgrounds they would *know* that," she explains. "We need to use a process that allows all applicants to feel they are able to represent themselves well."

NEHA SAMPAT, CEO of Contentstack, a pioneer and industry leader in omni-channel content management, was named to the Forbes Technology Council in 2017. In part because her company operates in both the US and India, she is particularly attuned to cultural issues as they affect female employees. "Family roles differ by culture," she explains, "so flexible working arrangements can be the key to making team members feel as if they have a level playing field."

Sampat also strongly suggests being alert for unconscious bias in the hiring process. "I have been amazed with the results I have seen when names are removed and replaced by an alias before applicant information is circulated to the hiring team members. It does make a measurable difference. And beyond that, it's crucial to create a culture where unconscious bias of any sort can be identified and called out."

TORSTEN KOLIND, who describes himself as "Danish at birth, European at heart," cofounded YouNoodle with Rebeca Hwang in 2010. Designed to connect startups with growth opportunities, the company is international in just about every way it's possible to be that way: leaders, employees, investors, operations. The staff represents 11 different countries. Kolind says he and his Co-founder had a head start in the inclusion arena because they came from three different continents: Europe, Asia and South America. As he puts it, that "kind of made it organic." When it isn't organic, he quickly adds, the leadership must create it. "Remember that adage," he says, "Culture eats strategy for breakfast." He is not in favor, however, of the kind of quotas some European countries have legislated for inclusion on corporate boards. Instead, inclusion must be a core value, born of corporate commitment.

REBECA HWANG, for her part, argues that: "People are not just one thing. I'm not just a woman, I'm not just an immigrant, I'm not just a mother. What's important to capture for real innovative, creative thinking is the degree of diversity we have in each individual." Her own history is a case in point. Born in Korea, she grew up in Argentina, studied Chemical Engineering as an undergrad at MIT (where she also cofounded the business accelerator named Cleantech Open), pursued a PhD at Stanford, and became Co-founder of Rivet Ventures after she served six years as CEO at YouNoodle. In an interview published by *Forbes* magazine in 2014,[9] she described a number of situations in which she is frequently ignored or engaged in personal instead of professional conversations because she is a woman, but at the same she pointed out that there are distinct advantages to being a woman executive, including but not limited to "You stand out."

DAVID JULIUS KING III was the Head of Diversity and Belonging at Airbnb when we conducted our interview. Today (2019) he serves in a similar capacity for Shopify, and carries the title of Head of Employee Experience, Diversity and Belonging. While he believes that inclusion is still not at the forefront of all too many companies' value set, and that there continue to be some who have not yet recognized that "inclusive teams are productive teams," once those hills are climbed and there is buy-in that this is all about optimal performance for investors and customers alike, there are ways to increase inclusion. The top on his list, especially for larger companies where it is not feasible to speak regularly with every employee, is the use of feedback surveys. If employees know these surveys are being taken seriously, and if they are taken seriously, he argues, results are measurable and the business metrics will show it.

RACHEL WILLIAMS, Global Head of Diversity at StubHub, dis-agrees with those who insist that there are plenty of candidates in the pipeline for those companies with the tenacity and purpose to find them. She adds, though, that the problem is what she calls "multi-layered." As she puts it, "The tech industry has not done a good job of marketing itself to these [marginalized] communities to get them interested in joining us here in Silicon Valley to help build the products they all use.... And our education system is not doing its job and graduating students of color." In the end though, she argues the problem has a solution, if school administrators, local government and corporations work together.

SURAJ SRINIVAS is all about education. As Co-founder and Chief Strategy Officer of Chalk.com, he leads an organization that finds efficiencies and connectivity for teachers, administrators and school systems. Like many others have stated in these interviews, he sees inclusion to be rooted in life experiences and the perspectives that derive from them as much as from any specific gender, age or social/economic group. "Innovation," he says simply, "is born at the intersection of different perspectives." And also like others, he notes that feeling safe and willing to take risks that might not succeed is a prerequisite for full expression and participation on the part of many who are operating in unfamiliar territory. "Everyone needs to know they have the opportunity to be heard. It reminds me, for example, of nurses from some cultures who have been taught that under no circumstances do they question the decision of a physician. Many immigrants are shy for similar reasons. The role of the CEO is to set up an environment in which everyone can be recognized and appreciated."

SAVITA VAIDHYANATHAN was still in office as Mayor of Cupertino, CA, when we conducted our interview, and the first person of Indian descent to serve in that office. After many years of being actively involved in her community and with her daughter's school activities, she eventually was elected President of the Rotary Club in Cupertino. She described her experience in a 2014 article in *India Currents* this way:

> While Indo-Americans are now well known for their technical prowess and sit on Boards of companies and Indian NPOs, it was not common to find them on local community Boards. In the early days, I was often mistaken as staff or tech support and had to work really hard to earn my place. Many a time, when we were introduced at Rotary events, people would assume that my husband was the President. I had to "lean in" and shake the extended hand.[10]

So, what she has felt and what she has witnessed both inform her ideas about inclusion. She has many, of course, but there are two that are particularly relevant:

1. On almost every level of education, girls are given the impression that some fields of investigation—and the professions for which they prepare one—are for boys only. That is the core reason why they are not attracted to STEM.

2. Immigration is, at base, a source of significant benefit to the community. Handled appropriately it will provide highly qualified workers with diverse experiences.

LAURA MATHER is the former CEO of Talent Sonar, a hiring platform designed to detect and control for unconscious bias and help companies build teams that are effective and innovative and reflect their core values. She identifies three issues that she believes stand in the way of employers' being able to consider the full spectrum of available talent:

1. Language choices in job descriptions and images on websites and promotional materials that can make some groups choose not to even apply;
2. Inequity when evaluating resumes, based on names or other indicators of race or gender; and
3. Unstructured and unskilled interviews.

Mather has multiple recommendations to address these issues, including the use of algorithms designed to detect such issues, removing names from resumes to be evaluated, and doing the research to determine which interviews are actually effective.

BILL IHRIE had retired from his position as Chief Technology Officer for Intuit when we interviewed him, but over his career he had worked not only in the technology world itself, but in a technology role for the banking industry. His experiences had made him keenly aware of the importance of being tuned in to customer needs and preferences in product development. "In my opinion, if you're developing a product for 20- to 30-year-olds, then a 25-year-old is likely to be a better product manager than a 45-year-old." And he applies the same rule in reverse. "Later in my career, I made it clear what I provided was context, not content," he remembers.

"By that time, coding languages and techniques being used by developers bore little resemblance to the ones I knew."

JAMES LATTIN is Professor of Marketing at the Stanford University Graduate School of Business, where his recent research has centered on consumer relationship management and loyalty or reward programs. Taking the "devil's advocate" position regarding the theory of diversity as part of our discussion, he warned against what he called "management by consensus." It is functional not, he argues, "when everyone agrees, but instead only when everyone agrees *after they have been heard and acknowledged by the group.*" He also points out that some hiring practices can have unintended consequences, not because of explicit discrimination toward one or another marginalized group, but because of too much adherence to a specific qualification or measurement. "Take intelligence: as we have already learned, there is cultural context that has been built in inadvertently that is disadvantageous to those who do not understand the context." And he concludes: "Team members would do well to learn and understand what it means 'to shine,' study the different ways they can move forward and aspire to great achievement based on what others accomplish."

MARICE BROWN has devoted the vast majority of her career to the banking industry. Since 2006, she has had leadership positions in private banking with J. P. Morgan Chase, in New York, California, Texas and now again New York as Head of Mexico, Private Bank. She believes strongly that the ability of women and other affected groups to advance is, indeed, improved by mentors and sponsors, but that is not enough. The "mentee" has a responsibility as well, in fact the primary responsibility. She bases that on personal experience as she puts it:

In 2013, I was 7 months pregnant with my second child and a management role opened in my team. There were men who were more senior than me who were interested in that role. I thought I had no chance to get it but after talking to my mentors and sponsors I decided to raise my hand anyway. I sat down with finance to learn about the new group, met with part of the team, and came up with a first 90 day plan of what I intended to do if I became Team Leader for that group. I sat down with the senior managers in charge of making the decision to explain my plan and why I thought I was the best candidate for the job and I got it. Having people supporting me was very important but being well prepared was key.

ALISON NICOLL was not sure whether she would stay in the US or return to her native Scotland when she entered Columbia Law School. It was with the help of one of her professors that she found her first job as a legal researcher for the Forced Migration Project of the Open Society Institute. Since then, her career trajectory has consistently focused on finance and investments, first in New York City and then in Silicon Valley. She served for six years as General Counsel at Paypal before moving to Upstart Network as General Counsel and Chief Compliance Officer.

An online lending platform, Upstart uses non-traditional measures to qualify individuals for loans, paying particular attention to compliance management. The measures, such things as academic performance and work history, signal the potential of loan applicants and can be especially helpful for new immigrants or those seeking funding to go to coding camps. "Traditionally, only about half the US population has access to term credit," explains Nicoll. "We are aware that our approach can be controversial, and very careful to both maintain a robust compliance program and avoid any unintended or unrecognized bias." Looks as if the door to the pipeline may be opening a bit more!

REED HASTINGS, CEO of Netflix, defines the top three topics of import to business leaders in mid-2019 (when we did our interview) as China, artificial intelligence, and what he calls DEI, for "diversity, equity and inclusion." He sees the inclusion issue as one that is seminal to any well-founded process of decision-making. "Yes, it's about gender, race, and all of those related issues, but it's more than that. Ours is a multi-local world, and a decision based on serving all 'locations' is healthier." Recalling his own experience in recruiting a CEO after having purchased Dreambox, he notes, "If we had stayed with the old boys' club, we would never have found Jesse Woolley-Wilson, and she's taken a startup from $1 million to $50 million."

From his experience serving on corporate boards (including Facebook and Microsoft), Hastings is all too aware of what he calls "social isolation," which arises when recruiting processes are not sufficiently inclusive. He credits his experience as a Crown Fellow (an Aspen Institute program) with helping him understand the value of a blinding in the interview process. "The focus on inclusion is way overdue," he insists. "For a while we are going to be scrambling to keep up, and the progress we are making is largely created by younger people."

JANICE ELLIG is quite clear about what she champions, and it's good corporate governance. As CEO of the Ellig Group, she has been named by *Business Week* as "one of the world's most influential headhunters," and she has a record of placing women and other affected group members in C-suite positions (75 percent) and boards (85 percent) that is hard to beat. Also the author of two books, in March 2019 she started a podcast channel entitled

"Leadership Reimagined," designed to present the stories of achieving women. "The research is irrefutable," she says. "Inclusive boards, even those with weaker skill-sets than their homogeneous counterparts, are more successful at leading in today's economy." She has little patience for those who complain about pipeline issues, and offers three specific strategies:

> First, if you're in touch with communities of skilled candidates with the profile you're looking for, you can find them. Second, sometimes you need to retrain the corporate decision-makers to open the aperture a bit wider. Who wants seven present and former CEOs sitting around the table, each trying to take charge? How about the candidate who has led a successful division or project? And finally, grooming internal candidates over time by having them work in various roles (let the CFO take over P&L) to let them learn the company minimizes disruption when the succession takes place and creates a better, more committed employee in the process. If it works for Best Buy and Apple, it can and will work for other strategic thinkers.

ENDNOTES

[1] David R. Francis, "Employers' Replies to Racial Names," www.nber.org/digest/sep03/w9873.html.

[2] Stephanie Thompson, "Here's Why You Didn't Get that Job: Your Name," www.weforum.org/agenda/2017/05/job-applications-resume-cv-name-discrimination/.

[3] Donna Ballman, "Can a Job Description Be Age Discrimination," www.forbes.com/sites/nextavenue/2017/05/10/can-a-job-rejection-be-age-discrimination/#cc37d23621a3.

[4] Jeffrey Dastin, *Amazon Scraps Secret AI Recruiting Tool that Showed Bias Against Women*, www.reuters.com/article/us-amazon-com-jobs-automation-insight/amazon-scraps-secret-ai-recruiting-tool-that-showed-bias-against-women-idUSKCN1MK08G.

[5] Amy Elisa Jackson, "Popular Companies Using AI to Interview and Hire You," www.glassdoor.com/blog/popular-companies-using-ai-to-interview-hire-you/.

[6] Hosanager, Kartik. *How Algorithms Are Shaping Our Lives and How We Can Stay in Control: A Human's Guide to Machine Intelligence.* Viking, New York: 2019.

[7] Donna Orem, "Addressing Implicit Bias in the Hiring Process," www.nais.org/magazine/independent-school/fall-2018/addressing-implicit-bias-in-the-hiring-process/.

[8] Rachel Thomas, Marianne Cooper, PhD, Ellan Konar, PhD, Megan Rooney, Mary Noble-Tolla, PhD, Ali Bohrer, Lareina Ye, Alexis Krivkovich, Irina Starikova, Kelsey Robinson, Marie-Claude Hadeau, and Nicole Robinson, PhD, "Women in the Workplace 2018," (LeanIn and McKinsey and Co., 2018) https://womenintheworkplace.com/.

[9] Denise Restauri, "What It's Like Being a Woman in Silicon Valley," https://www.forbes.com/sites/deniserestauri/2014/10/13/what-its-like-being-a-woman-in-silicon-valley/#65d050b82f21.

[10] Savitya Vaidhyanathan, "My Journey," https://indiacurrents.com/savita-vaidhyanathans-journey/.

CHAPTER SEVEN

Training the Trainers

—

The year was 2018. The place, a medical clinic in the Southeastern US specializing in cardiology. The patient, a female in her mid-70s, turned to the staffer leading her to a treatment room, and said, "I know you are much too young to realize this, but it is amazing and heartening to me that so many of the people who work here, including physicians, are female."

Quietly, the younger woman responded: "Don't get too excited. Your doctor is having a bit of a hill to climb. Not all medical specialties are alike, and male cardiologists, here at least, can be less than welcoming."

As we have worked on this book, it has become increasingly clear that bias is often implicit, and inclusion cannot be adequately assessed by merely assembling numbers and faces. When the subject is training, that can be especially true, because the word itself is most often thought to mean a kind of education aimed at those in middle and lower employment levels, certainly never at the occupants of the C-suite. The example above—a true story—captures that issue dramatically. Consider the situation that faces the employing company. Is it easy to imagine a workshop that addresses the issue head-on for the entire medical staff *including* physicians?

A quick check of the literature relating to inclusion in medical environments produces multiple studies and from them a host of viable recommendations. It is interesting to note, though, that while mentorship is mentioned, training rarely is. And at the same time, a study published on the *Journal of the American Medical Association* Open Network[1] notes that diversifying leadership isn't enough. It is important for administrators, leaders, and mentors to receive implicit bias training and to develop leadership skills that include how to respond to feedback.

Corporate America may not yet totally accept the premise that it, too, could face a similar issue. Indeed, the jury is still somewhat out on the effectiveness of training for inclusion and diversity, despite the growing numbers of consultancies in that line of business. One particularly comprehensive and regularly cited study was published by the Oxford Library of Psychology in 2013.[2] Authors Frank Dobbin and Alexandra Kalev argue that using training, performance evaluation and bureaucratic rules to foster inclusion and diversity has been "broadly ineffective." Mentoring, taskforces and giving staffers full-time positions devoted to the issue have been more successful.

Writing in *Time* magazine in 2018,[3] Joanne Lipman, whose career has included senior positions at *The Wall Street Journal*, Conde Nast and Gannett, among others and who may be best known for her book, *What She Said, What Men Need to Know (and Women Need to Tell Them)*, pointed to three ways that the Dobbin/Kalev study suggests training fails: when it's mandatory, if and when it mentions the law, or when it's only for managers and not for all employees. She goes on to add that companies nonetheless continue to spend almost $8 billion a year on such training.

The solution? Again according to Lipman, for many employers it is a variation focused on unconscious bias, at the time of her writing offered by two in ten companies in the US and expected quickly to increase to at least half. Why is it more effective? Lipman's argument is two-fold: (1) it is structured to be guilt-free; and (2) leaders are not just talking, but acting by offering such incentives as parental leave.

There is, of course, no real consensus that training programs are ineffective. Other studies argue otherwise. One of those, written by four psychology professors and published in the *Harvard*

Business Review,[4] suggests that reported effectiveness derives from a three-part combination: the choice of training method used, the personality characteristics of trainees, and just what outcomes are measured. They offer two specific recommendations.

The first is to include what they dub "perspective-taking," which is basically engaging in an exercise that makes the trainee walk in the shoes of someone who is different. The specific technique they used was an assignment to write a description of some of the challenges a marginalized group might face.

The second is goal-setting, such as an intent to challenge inappropriate comments rather than remain silent.

And, as we argued in the introduction to this book, it remains important—particularly so in training—to recognize that inclusion can be lethally compromised in what might be called the "reverse direction." In late 2017, journalist, entrepreneur and corporate trainer Joanne Cleaver wrote an article for the *Chicago Tribune*[5] detailing her experience with an online workshop that lasted a month and was supposed to help train white women to be supportive of women of color. One especially virulent exchange takes us back to the medical world. When the group saw a Facebook feed in which a white woman exulted over having graduated from medical school, the workshop attendees insisted her achievement was possible only because of her "whiteness." The new graduate's explanation that she had been a foster child and worked her way through undergraduate school failed to turn the tide. As the writer pointed out: "It's not a good sign when you discover that everybody in a diversity workshop thinks the same way." And after the experience, she added: "I'm not black, Latina, Asian or Native American, and I don't know what it's like to move through life initially defined by the color of my skin. But I know what it's like for people to judge me based on my appearance. I know it's not the same, but it's a start."

PERSPECTIVES ON POINT

Insights Gained from Personal Interviews by the Authors

MARIA WEAVER is Chief People Officer at Funding Circle, a company that creates growth internationally by linking businesses looking for financial support with investors—both individual and institutional, over 70,000 of them as this book is being written. With her leadership, Funding Circle has established processes for both hiring and training that focus on the power of inclusion. On the hiring front, the process identifies experience that is "practical and useful," and at the same time seeks what Weaver refers to as a "culture add" as opposed to a "culture fit." And once the hire is made, the company works to create a culture of its own that employees will consider a safe place. "We want our employees to bring their authentic selves to work—to be bold." When that same culture is focused on employee training, the company is careful about compliance, but also goes beyond "just don't do it," on issues such a sexual harassment. "The idea is to make our employees understand the complexities of issues such as this, and what the long-term implications are when mistakes are made."

TODD MANLEY, Senior Director, Corporate Development and Integration Management at Symantec, offers a perspective on inclusion that, while not precisely "unique," is shared by few in the business world. It may well speak to the issue of being sensitive to differences more directly than most others. As he puts it, "Most always, I am the tallest person in the room, and I try to be aware of the impact that is having, whether I mean for it to or not." He goes on to describe some tactics he has adopted as a result. "If I'm in a setting where consensus is important, and I realize that I'm head and shoulders about anyone else at the table, I look to see if I can lower my seat." He also notes that it is common for people to feel quite comfortable exclaiming "Man, you're tall!" Obviously, few would be quite so honest were the adjective "short" or "fat" or "dark" or "light." Another testimony to how loaded language can be, and how that "load" is culturally defined.

RICHARD PATTON, CEO and CIO of Courage Capital Management, LLC, which specializes in bankruptcies and other special situation investing, reports he has the obverse of Todd Manley's problem. "I'm short, so I have enough personal experience to know that people can be selective about almost anything. The point is simple: hire, include, promote, based on skill, not some country club mentality. If the process isn't blind, then the objective is poorly served because you risk missing the most qualified people."

FIDEL VARGAS at the age of 23 became the youngest person in the US to be elected Mayor of a major city, in his case Baldwin Park, CA. He has served on a number of private and public sector boards, was appointed to national advisory organizations by both Presidents Clinton and Bush, and named one of the US Top Young Leaders by *Time* Magazine. After having served in leadership positions and founded a number of investment companies over his career, he today is CEO and President of the Hispanic Scholarship Fund. With that kind of experience under his belt it is not surprising that he has very specific, defined ideas about how to harness the power of inclusion.

His approach includes multiple steps, all of them practically defined:

1. Identify senior roles for which there is an opportunity to practice inclusion, much like the NFL hires coaches.
2. Avoid doing business the way you always have and instead work toward finding and/or establishing connections between those who are responsible for talent acquisition and the individuals with the "talent."
3. Take a systematic approach to creating a workplace environment that is comfortable and accepting so that those with new insights are not merely present but ready to offer insights that may be different from the norm.
4. Establish a culture that appreciates, incubates, stimulates a quest for continuous learning.

GLORIA MOLINS founded Trip4real Experiences, S.L., a travel services company headquartered in Barcelona, in 2013. Airbnb acquired the company in 2016, and Molins now serves as Head of Global Launches there. Absolutely passionate about entrepreneurship and enlightened management, she tells us: "When managers realize that inclusion [She said "diversity," but this was a couple of years ago.] increases production and makes a team better, everyone will be in a better place." And, when it comes to training, she is at once enthusiastic and precise: " As a manager, I believe in hearing out your team, identifying the things they are thinking about—what worries them, what they want to share with you—and helping them with those issues."

GREG BECKER makes any idea of referring to a banker as a "starched shirt" show just how shallow that kind of idiom can be. He's been with Silicon Valley Bank for more than a quarter century, as President and CEO more than 8 years. His company:

1. annually publishes a report on startups in the US, UK, China and Canada and also one on women filling startup leadership roles;

2. uses its website to feature clients who succeed and explain how they achieve that success;

3. builds bridges for tech companies to work with emerging markets and across national borders.

Becker himself is all about big ideas. As he puts it: "There are a lot of companies out there that can be built with pretty simple ideas, but the ones that are the big, bold ones are really those formed from big, bold transformative ideas. You can look at Uber, Airbnb, WeWork. The aspirations of those entrepreneurs are truly about building something completely different and leveraging technology in an incredible way."

GERMAN TEOBALDO JIMENEZ VEGA earned his MBA in 2003 from the Sloan School of Management at MIT and has since held a series of senior management positions in the oil industry. As of this writing he is Vice President for Pluspetrol in Argentina. He sees his career trajectory as having been heavily influenced by mentors. "The first and most important," he stresses, "is my own mother. And then the encouragement and advice, plus the vision of what can and cannot be done I learned during my university experience, continue to be important influences."

JUDITH KLEINBERG has a front-row seat when it comes to understanding the complexities of finding, training and hiring a skilled workforce. Formerly Mayor of Palo Alto and currently CEO of the city's Chamber of Commerce, she brings to the table a diverse and active career advising and managing startups, acting as legal counsel, serving on both corporate and not-for-profit boards—the list goes on. She is precise and analytical when she describes how a community, such as Palo Alto, where housing is prohibitively expensive and public transportation less than effective, struggles to deal with pipeline issues. "The situation is truly complex," she says. "On the one hand, people who could and would like to be part of the skilled workforce cannot afford either to live here or to live close enough that their travel is not a drain on productivity and eventually a cause for burnout. On the other hand, we continually have organizations setting up innovation centers here, because they recognize that this is, essentially, a center of talent and potential." Kleinberg's suggested approach (and one she is striving to put into place) is to "create sustainable social change and community vitality, and from that derive a good business climate."

MO FATHELBAB is as good an example as you're likely to find of someone who developed a skill set as part of a job, came to enjoy what he was doing and to see that it really was making a difference in the lives of business leaders and the success of their enterprises, realized it could easily become full-time and started his own—you're filling in the blank already with "consulting firm." Not exactly. Not even mostly. Fathelbab's company, Forum Resources Network, trains peer exchange groups (more often than not CEOs) to use interpersonal skills in a confidential, collaborative session to essentially "mentor" each other. To be honest, this may be the paradigm of peer-to-peer collaboration, built not on the assumption that Person Δ is more skillful than Person $\lozenge$, but instead on the understanding that if Person Δ has had an experience that will help Person $\lozenge$ with a challenge s/he is facing, there's a chance to not only share that experience, but to let others in the group participate as well. Because participants (Fathelbab's team have worked with more than 20,000 so far.) in the Forum experience see and benefit from its strength, many choose to use what they've learned to establish the kind of corporate culture that nurtures inclusion.

STEVE BENNETT, former CEO of Intuit, (See Perspectives in Chapter 5 for more detail.) created a significant increase in revenue during his tenure. We asked him to what he attributes that achievement. He explains:

> Our strategy statement was "Being in a Good Business with Strategies to Succeed and Talented and Engaged Employees Delighting Customers." The way to do that is to create a great place to work that will mobilize employees to produce great results for customers, which in turn means more rewards for shareholders. Some people put that in reverse order, but to me it's employees first, which of course requires lots of leadership development and training. Most growth is organic.

CAROLINE WINNETT in essence works with one foot in the classroom and the other in the boardroom. As Executive Director of Berkeley Skydeck, the premier startup accelerator at UC Berkeley, she has literally (from the third floor of the university's tallest building) and figuratively a bird's-eye view of 100 startups, and works with more than 150 mentors assigned to enrich the business-leadership development that grows companies. In our interview we asked her what she thought society might do in the future to advance inclusion in the workplace. She answers in two ways. On the practical level—one business at a time—she suggests that all too often those who are earnestly trying to be inclusive are completely unconscious of the ways they are failing to do so. "The statistics now show that startups that focus on embracing the contributions of what I like to call 'unincluded groups' outperform those that don't, so it's not hard to sell the idea," she explains, "but they often just don't realize implicit bias. Coaching is crucial." On a more theoretical note, she points out that "the brain is hardwired to include what is familiar." That means, of course, that creating experiences and environments that expand horizons will over time create change. "We need to be relentless, yet patient," Winnett concludes.

BUNNY SUMNER YOUNG founded a business that harnesses her skills as a coach, a trainer, a therapist, a motivational speaker, a producer of make-it-happen workshops, and a mental health professional. It's called "A Better Place Consulting," and the history behind it is as much one of personal determination as it is of professional drive. At the age of 14, Young was diagnosed with a heart condition. "That's the kind of experience that makes you take stock," she says. She took a fistful of meds on a daily basis, and it wasn't until she was 17 that a physician asked her if she really liked taking meds. "I didn't know there was an alternative," she remembers, "and when she suggested a service animal, I protested that I was neither hearing- nor sight-impaired. Like so many people, I had no real understanding of service animals, what they are trained to do, and how the system works." She relates that experience now to what many business leaders and prospective business founders she has counseled face. "If you have never run a company, you don't know what you don't know" is the way she phrases it. And she adds that solving that problem effectively happens when everyone involved in an enterprise feels safe and accepted enough to be honest and innovative without fear of rejection or derision.

Young's continuing experience with a service dog regularly sheds light on the issues that devolve when an individual is somehow different, and no open conversations have taken place to bring down the barriers that can exist. "I actually had one man ask me if I had a saddle he could use to ride my dog," she says. "And one of my employers, without talking with me first, suggested that folks 'come in to meet our company dog,' while another insisted I leave the dog at home because of an event we had scheduled." Clearly, there is inclusion, but there is also intrusion and delusion.

"So many people don't really know where to start finding a better or a different way to do business," Young concludes. The two elements she focuses on for productive, successful business models are: (1) a safe environment created to encourage employees to "bring their whole selves to work"; and (2) a collaborative consciousness, which she defines as entrepreneurs working as a "tribe," because "we're better together."

ROSHNI NAIDU originally joined the staff at Amazon just after earning her Master's Degree in Financial Engineering and Risk Analytics at Rensselaer Polytechnic Institute. Four years later she interrupted her tenure to earn an MBA at the Wharton School, and today she is Senior Technical Product Manager for Amazon. Also having participated in multiple internship programs, she is keenly aware of the importance of training, mentorship, and especially sponsorship. "Yes, there are hills to climb when you don't look like anyone else in the room," she affirms, "and I have been extremely lucky to have more senior women in meetings offer to act as mentors for me. Because of that, I in turn make those offers to women who have less experience than I do." She also stresses that she finds sponsors even more important. "To me," she explains, "a mentor helps you grow, whereas a sponsor is the person at the table who is willing to stick her or his neck out for you, tell you about the new opportunities, tell decision-makers about your skills, do everything possible to make it happen for you." As a result, she adds, she works extra hard to live up to the portrait the sponsor has painted. She recognizes clearly that the responsibilities that rest on the person being helped are just as great as those of the person helping. It's not surprising to learn that her Wharton MBA class recommended her for the "Benji Shuttler" award for selfless leadership—or that she won it.

PATTI PEREZ is a woman on a mission. Her goal, as she describes it on her LinkedIn profile is "to create a revolutionary shift in the way we communicate and make decisions at work." Thus far, she has found a multitude of ways to pursue that goal: attorney, state regulator, HR pro, speaker, trainer, and, now, author. Her current book, *The Drama-Free Workplace: How to Prevent Unconscious Bias, Sexual Harassment, Ethics Lapses and Inspire a Healthy Culture* hits the major issues head-on and her work as Vice President of Workplace Strategy for Emtrain, a workplace culture technology firm, offers daily opportunities for her to advocate for what she believes in by helping companies build inclusive cultures. In our interview, she is direct in describing what it takes for leaders to truly build healthy workplace cultures. "One way to approach it," she explains, "is to see the process as having three layers:

1. Are we really ready to say these issues are important?
2. How about ok with spending the money it takes?
3. Have we taken the time and effort to see that the money is put to effective use?"

Perez is particularly focused on that last point. "It's too easy to just 'throw money' at the issues, a little like wealthy parents throw money at spoiled kids. If a company's platform and mission are not about democratizing their culture and reflective of the need for social justice, the money makes little difference."

ENDNOTES

[1] Jaya Aysola, MD, DRM&H, MPH; Frances K. Barg, PhD, MEd; Ana Bonilla Martinez, BS, CHES; et al, "Perceptions of Facotrs Associated with Inclusive Work and Learning Environments in Health Care Organizations: A Qualitative Narrative Analysis," https://jamanetwork.com/journals/jamanetworkopen/fullarticle/2695077 doi:10.1001/jamanetworkopen.2018.1003.

[2] Dobbin, F, and A Kalev. 2013. "The Origins and Effects of Corporate Diversity Programs," pp. 253-281 in Oxford Handbook of Diversity and Work, edited by QM Roberson. New York: Oxford University Press.

[3] Joanne Lipman, "How Diversity Training Infuriates Men and Fails Women," http://time.com/5118035/diversity-training-infuriates-men-fails-women/.

[4] Alex Lindsey, Eden King, Ashley Membere, and Ho Kwan Cheung *Two Types of Diversity Training That Really Work*. https://hbr.org/2017/07/two-types-of-diversity-training-that-really-work.

[5] Joanne Cleaver, "Commentary: I Got Kicked Out of Diversity Training," https://www.chicagotribune.com/news/opinion/commentary/ct-perspec-diversity-feminism-white-privilege-20171217-story.html.

CHAPTER EIGHT

Politics and Policy

—

The intersection between the corporate world and public policy in the United States has perennially been problematic at best, and often even fractious. Traditionally, of course, corporate America's effect on public policy is played out in terms of: (1) donations, which are closely regulated on the federal level and often accomplished largely through Political Action Committees (PACs); (2) lobbyists; and (3) membership in trade associations that hire registered lobbyists and otherwise seek to inform the political process. According to the The Center for Responsive Politics, in 2018, there were 11,586 lobbyists in the US, and lobbying spending reached $3.42 billion.[1]

Participation on the state and local levels varies widely by jurisdiction, as well as by where and how corporations do business. It is on that level, though, that the most direct effect on the issue of inclusion in the workplace has played out in the 21st century. In September 2018, California Governor Jerry Brown signed into law a bill requiring any corporation with shares listed on a major US stock exchange and having a principal executive office in that state to appoint at least one female director on its board by the end of 2019. Further, for any of those companies with a board of five directors, two must be female by the end of 2021. With six or more directors, the number becomes at least three.[2]

Until that law was passed, the pressure for inclusion on corporate boards had come largely from the adjudication of court cases and the policies of institutional investors. In its "Fearless Girl" campaign, for example, State Street in 2018 voted against re-election of nominating and governance committee directors at more than 500 companies judged to have failed to make a creditable effort to address the inclusion issue.[3] BlackRock also began in 2017 to push for board inclusion as well as pay more attention to issues such as wage equity.[4]

The message from all of this? Wise corporate managers realize that dealing with inclusion issues not just once, but over time is beginning to have direct and measurable influence on all kinds of financial indicators.

DEMOGRAPHY DIRECTS THE DIALOGUE

As this book is being written (mid-2019), the minds of Americans, and in many cases their emotions, are being consumed by the issue of immigration, especially as it relates to those coming from Central and South America. While we differ starkly in age and in the amount of time we have spent in the US corporate community, both of your authors moved to the US from Peru. We are keenly aware that our national perspectives are not exactly "diverse," and also acknowledge that using statistics or projections to address the turmoil surrounding immigration could well render this book anachronistic by the time you will be reading it. So, instead, we are choosing to make two basic points:

1. The "half-life" of emotions produced by any us-and-them mentality is a good bit longer than that of the basic issues that produce those emotions.

2. Insofar as any immigration policy has a negative effect on the ability of children in America to be appropriately

educated and assimilated into the social order, corporations and the nation itself will pay a steep price.

Us and Them: We dealt briefly earlier in this book with the behavior that evolves—maybe better said, "erupts"—when a person is defined as the "other," even if that definition is based on as little as the way someone dresses, talks or gestures, or whether she or he has been artificially assigned to a group without any behavior or belief having justified that assignment. (One is assumed to be racist because he lives in Alabama or elitist because she attended Harvard University.) One way that corporations have chosen to address this "otherness" is to form affiliations with a wide variety of culture-based community groups. McDonalds, for example, lists more than 15 "key partners" representing a full array of membership profiles: women, black, Asian, Hispanic, American Indian, etc.[5] Taking a step further, the company sets up what it calls "Employee Business Networks" through which employees can find mentors, sponsors and role models, and have access to senior leadership. (See multiple references to other companies that do the same throughout this book.)

Bill Coleman describes the employee groups at Veritas as central to the company's culture of inclusion. In that case there are eight such groups—the one for women is known as WAVE (Women at Veritas Empowered) and operates not just in the US, but in Veritas installations worldwide. In the community, Veritas also sponsors programs in collaboration with historically black colleges, as well as with veterans groups, to name just two.

How does this relate to public policy? If and when political wrangling undercuts government-sponsored programs or in other ways isolates immigrants, corporate leaders sensitive to the power of inclusion can and will take up the slack, as will community leaders in the growth of local commerce.

This becomes an even stronger avenue to pursue when we consider the fact that immigrants are strongly represented among the self-employed. According to a Pew Research report[6] the percentages of self-employed immigrants vs. US-born by ethnic group in 2014 were as follows:

	IMMIGRANT	NATIVE BORN
Asian	11 percent	7 percent
Black	7 percent	5 percent
Hispanic	11 percent	6 percent
White	17 percent	11 percent

Education: The complexion of the 2019 workforce in the US is described quite differently, depending on the argument the analyst, speaker, writer, journalist, politician is seeking to make. Some point to low unemployment rates. Others insist that those calculations are misleading, because so many individuals who are able and would like to be employed have given up seeking a job, and they are not being counted as "unemployed."

Similarly, some argue that jobs are being exported because taxes and other governmental programs render employment costs prohibitive and give corporations little choice. Others say corporate leaders are so eager to maximize profit margins at any cost that they are willing to destroy communities and decimate the working class by exporting any unskilled jobs they can, plus those that require just basic skills.

Those with the vision to look ahead a decade or so realize that these disputes could well be overshadowed by large-scale displacement of workers unless planning begins now. It can be argued that there is a "perfect storm" of sorts brewing on the horizon, created by the conjunction of:

1. the prospect of AI, drones, robots and other technological advances taking over many positions now filled by manufacturing and administrative workers;
2. the skyrocketing costs of higher education, so that those without the money to go beyond the secondary school level either forego the opportunity to improve their access to better jobs or teeter under debt loads that severely limit how and when they can purchase homes and otherwise participate in what some predict to be an expanding consumer society;
3. rising income inequality, especially in the US and China.

In their 2017 report entitled "Jobs Lost, Jobs Gained: Workforce Transitions in Times of Automation,"[7] researchers for the McKinsey Global Institute suggest that by 2030 between 75 million and 375 million members of the global workforce will face the need to switch occupational categories. They stress that this is a scenario that describes not a lack of available jobs, but a *change* in the jobs available. As they put it:

> Increased investment and productivity growth from automation could spur enough growth to ensure full employment, but only if most displaced workers find new work within one year.... To achieve good outcomes, policymakers and business leaders will need to embrace automation's benefits, and, at the same time, address the worker transitions brought about by these technologies.

At the close of 2018 *The Star*,[8] Canada's largest daily newspaper, reprinted a prediction Isaac Asimov had written in 1983 about the year 2019. In discussing computerization, Asimov insisted that technological advance had historically created more jobs than it destroyed, but that the jobs especially in this case would be different, and a "vast change in the nature of education" would be required.

No statistics are needed to get agreement for the argument that entry-level positions are held disproportionately by women, black males, and the ethnic groups often lumped together as "minorities," despite the increase in their numbers. Arming these people with appropriate skills *before* they are displaced has already become a priority. A 2018 report published by the National Skills Coalition[9] notes that roughly 53 percent of the jobs in the US labor market qualify as "middle skill," (requiring education beyond high school, but not a college degree), and only 43 percent of workers have that kind of training.

A number of collaborative efforts between corporate and community college leaders are already bearing fruit on this front. At the same time, education-related trade associations are stepping up. According to The National Council for Workforce Education,[10] an affiliate of the American Association of Community Colleges, there are about 650,000 credentials, including traditional degrees, training programs and skill-based certifications already available in the US, and more and more community colleges and employers are promoting the concept of work-based learning.

The actual severity of income inequality in the US is a moving target, at best, and with enough time and a reasonably adept ability to use a search engine, you can come up with the kind of statistic that begins a good keynote speech—and support it. What matters in terms of inclusion, though, is not so much *how many* people are affected, as *how* they are affected. In 2014, the OECD (Organization for Economic Cooperation and Development)[11] found that among its member countries over the previous three decades, income inequality had:

- produced a statistically significant negative impact on economic growth, largely attributable to the gap between low-income households and the rest of the population;

- depressed skills development for citizens whose parents had limited education, both in terms of how much formal education they received and any improvement in skill efficiency.

Based on their findings, the researchers called for labor market policies that would promote employment for disadvantaged groups, plus offer childcare support and in-work benefits.

Finally, all of the above research applies not completely but largely to those without advanced education or demonstrable skills above the norm. That leaves out an important group. In 2018 a team of Stanford University researchers[12] amassed a wealth of data on the contributions immigrants have made in this country to innovation. Three will suffice here:

1. From 1990 through 2000, they account for 26 percent of the country's Nobel Prize winners.

2. Immigrants generate roughly ¼ the innovative output (measured by patents awarded, weighted citations they received and the economic value they produced) in the chemical, computers and communications, drugs and medical, and electronics sectors.

3. Immigrant inventors tend to have more collaborators than their native counterparts do.

(There is information in Chapter 5 to flesh out this argument.)

Again, how does this relate to public policy? Obliquely, perhaps, but importantly. Without the significant contribution of these individuals, the US could experience what one NIH researcher called a "brain drain." He explained that in his lab it was not unusual to have a team of top scientists from all over the world. Yes, he said, they might be drawn to this country because of access to superior funding, but what they talked about was the opportunity to work with others on their intellectual level, who had had significantly different life and educational experiences and because of it brought different contributions to the analyses.

Or, in other words, he was witnessing the positive version of us and them, that could well be lost if immigration policy somehow limits access or economic policy limits funding.

PERSPECTIVES ON POINT

Insights Gained from Personal Interviews by the Authors

JOE SIMITIAN is a consummate politician, and to us, as we write this, that does not have the "ring" that it should, because few in the political arena are garnering much respect. In Simitian's case, though, there are a string of awards, and too many public recognitions to list that together bolster the case that he, law degree in hand and the community good at heart, knows how political leadership can and does work to the benefit of all. Currently Santa Clara County Supervisor, he has taken a path through public service that arms him with personal experience in and around all sorts of cultures: state senator and assembly member, mayor of Palo Alto, multiple school board roles, election observer/supervisor in El Salvador and Bosnia, and volunteer for International Rescue Committee relief and resettlement programs in Albania and Kosovo. In other words, his opinions are based on broad experience. What is called for, he argues, is "transitional pathways" for immigrants. That means: (1) Being aware that we aren't attuned to their needs any better than they are attuned to our habits; (2) Recognizing skills even if they are not accompanied by American documentation; (3) Not just attracting the best and the brightest, but keeping them.

ALEX EPSTEIN deals in alternatives—ideas, organizations, approaches, philosophy, interpretations of history, and communication. It has been almost a decade since he founded the Center for Industrial Progress, (CIP) a for-profit think tank which takes as its core mission the recognition and use of human potential to improve our lives and our planet by judicious use of technology. His book, *The Moral Case for Fossil Fuels*, is precisely what its title proclaims it to be—an argument *for* the use of fossil fuels. Most of his work centers on energy use and climate science (or presumed science), but he also has adroitly articulated ideas about human potential. And he has developed what he calls an "extreme clarity tool" which is a means of getting people to agree with a position that you hold—let's say for inclusion—when they hold another. The approach he recommends involves explaining the other person's ideas "better than they can," by adding to, subtracting from and modifying the context. Heady stuff, and doing it justice would take another chapter or two, but when Epstein considers the common use of "diversity" and uses his method he sees it as an inexact term without clear differentiation of meaning or purpose. Affording someone an opportunity *because* he or she is a member of a certain race or because you need someone of that race instead of because you need that person on your team is, well, racism, he argues. Think about it.

CARL GUARDINO has served for more than two decades as President and CEO of the Silicon Valley Leadership Group, a public policy trade organization representing 350+ of the area's employers. He also holds leadership positions in the transportation and housing arenas, having been appointed to four consecutive terms on the California Transportation Commission and co-created Housing Trust Silicon Valley. And then there are a host of charitable organizations and events in which he is involved. Having dealt for many years with economic and social issues, he has a comprehensive understanding of the conjunction of private and public policy initiatives in a technology-rich environment. "It is much easier," he says, "to forecast demographic changes over the next decade than technological changes." In the face of a rapid increase in the number of Latino children in the area's school system, he expresses concern. "What we have realized is that we are failing most of our Latino children," he explains. "Today in Silicon Valley, only 59 percent of all our third-graders are reading at grade level, and for Latino children that number is even lower—35 percent." And in terms of potential solutions for social and economic imbalance, he says: "Our community colleges can play an integral role in our efforts to diversity our workforce and rebuild our middle class."

PAUL BRADLEY, Chairman and CEO of Caprica International, has had a career that belies belief. He has worked in a variety of corporate organizations, in public service roles (including for former U.S. Senator Paul Laxalt's office and the British House of Commons), in various senior management roles in the Far East— the list seems all but endless. When he lived and worked in Hong Kong, it was for a leading Japanese company, which rendered him a minority in two different ways (both to the Japanese and Hong Kong Chinese), an experience he describes as transformational. How did he learn to adapt? He remembers:

> When I went to Thunderbird School of Global Management, there were 85 nationalities in my class, so I had that early advantage of learning how to adapt across different cultures. When I was introduced to a different culture, I did everything I could to try to be culturally sensitized, to remember that it's not just what you say, but how you say it. With the Japanese, for example there are many kinds of subtle nuances around how you use body language to

show respect. You never pour your own drink, but pour the drink of others at the table. In India, I watched movies with English subtitles, studied the religion, the food and lifestyle to demonstrate my appreciation of their unique culture. In China, I would try all of the local food, learn to sing Mandopop karaoke songs, read the history and visit key heritage sites. I strongly believe that working across 14 countries has been an amazing gift. I have come to know that the strongest organization, the one with the competitive edge, is the one that blends the unique skills, cultures, nationalities, and perspectives together to create a dynamic entity. Leading a multi-cultural organization is an invaluable learning experience that changes you personally. You have to "jump to the other side" to have a multi-cultural perspective.

TERESA DAVIES is, by her own description, all about what she refers to as "impact." Impatient with anyone who describes a core value and is unable to point to tangible results or dollars invested to support that claim, she lives what she believes. Currently pursuing a Master's Degree in Public Affairs and Policy Analysis, she is also an active management consultant. When we interviewed her, she was still working in the energy industry—she has held senior positions in a number of Fortune 500 companies—and busy representing veterans in both community and corporate settings. A Navy veteran herself, she is one of those women who in multiple situations has been the "one of three" or the "only," be it woman, Latina or veteran. "Yes," she remembers, "I had a seat at the table, but I soon came to realize that did not necessarily mean my ideas were being heard, much less listened to." She found, as many others have, that location matters, and in ways that are sometimes surprising. For example, she witnessed more inclusion in San Diego than in San Francisco, and because the Indiana community she worked in was smaller than either of those she found her voice was much more likely to be heard "as long as I knew what I was talking about and could provide something that would affect the bottom line." Her work with the Service-Disabled Veteran-Owned Business Organization in that community opened up almost $60 million for veterans in less than year. "Being an outsider was a benefit," she insists. "That experience made me wonder if we are limiting ourselves by keeping to our own kind. It's important to know exactly what you want to do, have goals and be authentic. If you make a mistake, say so. Own your own limitations."

THAIS REZENDE draws from experience in a number of different fields when she designs initiatives to encourage and support entrepreneurship and business development. She has been a journalist working in both television and print media, a public relations professional, the lead developer of a business propulsion program (SuccessLink), a member of the staff of the Mexican Consulate, Program Developer for the Women's Initiative for Self Employment and then Executive Director of that organization's San Francisco and Marin County office. She then moved to the East Bay office, assuming the same leadership role. Since she became CEO of Bizworld.org, the group has greatly expanded its international reach.

Rezende shares with Bizworld.org Founder Tim Draper the vision that engaging elementary and middle school children in hands-on programs that focus on leadership, financial responsibility and teamwork helps them discover their own talents, develop critical skills, and build self-confidence. As they work together to create a business they are not only preparing themselves to take on academic challenges, but also to develop the kind of competency that feeds entrepreneurship. Since children are "optimists at heart," Bizworld sets the stage for "real world changes." In her opinion, though, skills and intelligence are only the start. "Success is based on opportunity."

ORIANA BRANON (CAMACHO) brings professional experience at some of the nation's largest public relations firms to her position as Alaska Airlines Director of Community and Public Relations for the San Francisco Bay Area. She is at once candid and convincing in her description of the company's approach to finding ways to support and enrich the community, especially for those residents whose access to education and career development may be limited. "No, we don't have the budgets that some of the larger airlines have," she admits, "but we are quite deliberate in trying to identify programs that produce tangible results." For example, she cites summer education programs such as "coding camps," where meals are provided and skills are developed for and among those who might not be able to afford more traditional advanced education programs. "Also," she adds, "we make an extra effort to be sure that the entire community is aware of job opportunities and career options where potential annual salaries may near $100,000 and the current talent pool is aging. Aviation mechanics is a prime example." Overall, the message she and her team wish to send is that "Alaska Airlines cares, we're here to stay, and we're growing."

KEN MCNEELY, CEO of AT&T West, is only partially joking when he refers to his company as a "140-year-old startup." Having begun his employment at AT&T in 1981 as an in-house attorney, he has both witnessed and participated in what can happen when corporate leaders look to the future informed by a full understanding of the community they serve and a commitment to accomplishing social good as well as meeting societal needs. He puts it simply: "The more you include, the better you innovate."

McNeely relates one story that is a particularly effective example of his argument.

> Silicon Valley and the Central Valley are geographically only about 50 miles apart, but culturally and economically they are worlds apart. We as a company decided it was important to help provide educational opportunities for the children of migrant workers in the Central Valley, and extended that to a program that not only included mentoring, but encouraged these young people to build cases for new products and services. One student's case was an eye-opener. It turns out that the workers wanted to pay their bills in cash, but couldn't because they were working during the hours of operation of our retail outlets. This student presented the case for a kiosk outside the store that is cash friendly, language friendly, and open all hours. It was one of those instances in which "we didn't know what we didn't know." Those kiosks are still in operation today.

As an African-American and a representative of the LGBT community, McNeely is also able to identify personal experiences during his nearly three decades at AT&T when his life perspective has helped in such arenas as brand awareness. It is not surprising that AT&T was awarded the Number One spot on DiversityInc's Top 50 Companies for Diversity list in 2019.

FRANK BAXTER believes that human beings are "hard-wired not to change our minds," and because of that in a series of situations has made it his business to try to understand the minds of others and see what kind of change that generates, for him and for those others. As the CEO of Jefferies Group LLC before his retirement in 2000 (He is Chairman Emeritus of Jefferies and Co now.) he adopted a distinctive management style he explains this way: "Once we'd decided on a mission, I didn't tell the management team what I wanted them to do or how to do it. Instead, I asked them what they planned, and then held them accountable for executing that plan. I think if you look at the company's performance the last decade of the 20th century, you will agree that something was working well."

Appointed to serve as US Ambassador to Uruguay by President George W. Bush, he quickly identified a tutor and began to learn Spanish. When he arrived in Uruguay, he found another, and the two continue to work together today via Skype. He remembers one particular experience from that tour of duty quite clearly. "My political position was a subject of real derision from some of the media. When I first arrived I was described as a 'Wall Street shark.'" Soon thereafter, the country suffered a natural disaster, the US sent financial support, and Baxter was given a script in English to read in order to explain the US gift. When he read the script in Spanish written to hand out to the local media, he insisted he could and would read that instead. "The fact that I spoke in Spanish was bigger news the next day than the gift was," he chuckles. That changed attitudes and reportage. Baxter obviously knows the value of including and being included.

NANCY BROWN has worked for the American Heart Association for more than 30 years and served as CEO for more than a third of that time. That experience has taught her that it is not only possible but productive, for an organization to be national in scope and "local" in impact. "For decades, AHA has focused on making sure that all people have access to health and well-being," she points out, "and also on creating an environment in which everyone is invited to be part of the process, whatever their professional, personal or economic background may be." In terms of innovation, she notes that AHA is an organization that is scientific, global, health-related and community-based. Its Social Impact Fund, established in 2018, is developing community based solutions, designed by local organizations to address social determinants of health. "We bring what we are good at to support what they are good at" is the way Brown describes it. And within the leadership of the organization, there is a strong commitment to promote inclusion. "For years, our board has recognized that when we focus on inclusion, our dialogue and outlook are richer and our perspectives are better," she concludes.

ENDNOTES

[1] www.opensecrets.org/lobby/.

[2] Howard Dicker, Lyuba Goltser and Erika Kaneko, Weil, Gotshal & Manges LLP, "Mandated Gender Diversity for California Boards," corpgov.law.harvard.edu/2018/10/18/mandated-gender-diversity-for-california-boards/.

[3] Lubya Goltser and Erika Kaneko, "State Street Escalates Policy on Board Gender Diversity and Touts Impact of its 'Fearless Girl' Campaign," https://governance.weil.com/latest-thinking/state-street-escalates/.

[4] "Blackrock Vows New Pressure on Climate, Board Diversity," Reuters, www.cnbc.com/2017/03/13/blackrock-vows-new-pressure-on-climate-board-diversity.html.

[5] https://corporate.mcdonalds.com/corpmcd/about-us/diversity-and-inclusion.html.

[6] http://www.pewsocialtrends.org/2015/10/22/immigrants-contributions-to-job-creation.

[7] James Manyika, Susan Lund, Michael Chui, Jacques Bughin, Jonathan Woetzel, Parul Batra, Ryan Ko, and Saurabh Sanghvi, "Jobs Lost. Jobs Gained, Workforce Transition in Times of Automation," (McKinsey Global Institute, 2017). www.mckinsey.com/~/media/mckinsey/featured%20insights/future%20of%20organizations/what%20the%20future%20of%20work%20will%20mean%20for%20jobs%20skills%20and%20wages/mgi-jobs-lost-jobs-gained-report-december-6-2017.ashx

[8] Isaac Asimov, "35 Years Ago, Isaac Asimov Was Asked by The Star to Predict the World of 2019. Here Is What He Wrote," www.thestar.com/news/world/2018/12/27/35-years-ago-isaac-asimov-was-asked-by-the-star-to-predict-the-world-of-2019-here-is-what-he-wrote.html..

[9] Katie Brown, "Powerful Partners: Businesses and Community Colleges," (National Skills Coalition, 2018) www.nationalskillscoalition.org/resources/publications/file/Powerful-Partners-Businesses-and-Community-Colleges.pdf.

[10] https://www.ncwe.org/page/2019_conference.

[11] https://read.oecd-ilibrary.org/social-issues-migration-health/trends-in-income-inequality-and-its-impact-on-economic-growth.

[12] Shai Bernstein, Rebecca Diamond, Timothy McQuade and Beatriz Pousada, "The Contribution of High-Skilled Immigrants to Innovation in the United States," (Stanford University, 2018). web.stanford.edu/~diamondr/bdmp_oct2018.pdf.

CHAPTER NINE

Trading Skills and Experience

—

First, let's address why this chapter is the penultimate one. While we differ in age and, quite naturally, in the generational attitude-sets that age defines, we both believe strongly that the facts, research, opinions, strategies and tactics we've presented so far in this book find their most direct application in personal relationships.

In a lot of ways, the situation is circular: inclusion begins with personal relationships, grows or wanes through personal relation-ships, and affects the workplace, the community, and even the economy as those personal relationships are enriched or rein-forced. We learn to be inclusive most readily by getting to know those who are different from us, in whatever way that is defined. The understanding we gain changes our behavior. That, in turn, prompts new reactions, attitudes and behaviors throughout the people and places that define our "world." As Henry Ford put it: "Coming together is a beginning. Keeping together is progress. Working together is success."

In the business "world," personal relationships are typically for-malized in two ways: team-building and mentoring. Let's take a look.

GO TEAM!

Might as well admit it. For teams—how to build them...how to select and train the members...whether to start with the project and then find the team to carry it out or present the goal, name the team and let the members define the project parameters—there are lots of competent and creative consultants ready to help and multiple frameworks in which to work. Essentially, inclusion is both the question and the answer.

Author and Stanford University Professor Tina Seelig (See Perspectives in Chapter 5 for full professional information.) has written widely on the importance of team interaction and how it is informed by careful inclusion of different points of view. In one podcast entitled "Tip Your Hat to Your Team"[1] published by Stanford University's eCorner, she reviews Edward deBono's "Six Hats Model," which uses different-colored hats to identify different roles people play:

- Those who focus on **facts** wear the white hat.
- Those who focus on **process** wear the blue hat.
- Those who lead with **creativity** wear the green hat.
- Those who rely heavily on their **intuition** wear the red hat.
- Those who see where things might **go wrong** wear the black hat.
- Those who focus on getting everyone to **get along** wear the yellow hat.

When Selig uses the model in her classroom, she gives students real hats with different-colored tassels, and lets them discover their comfort levels with different roles, how there is an optimal order within which the hats function, based on the task, etc. She concludes: "Teamwork is incredibly important when you are building organizations that are tackling thorny problems. You need a group composed of individuals who bring different perspectives to the table, who respect different working styles, and can tap into the value that each one brings."

It has become a truism to proclaim that the more inclusive the team, the more innovative the process. Inclusion not only produces a lively cross-fertilization of ideas, but sets the stage for creating a wider customer base and lays the groundwork for a quicker, richer and more lasting buy-in of entrepreneurial ideas. And, as is obvious from Seelig's work, inclusion involves not only the visible, but the intellectual, emotional and ideational.

Inclusion works best, in fact we believe works *only*, when team members engage in effective communication. The careful use of words and idioms, gestures, and body language, and whether team-member exchange is face-to-face or practiced through one or another written, audio or video technological channel are the issues central to effective collaboration. The research devoted to this subject could make for a book on its own, (and there are several comprehensive ones) so for our purposes here, we're going to present just one or two examples in each category.

Language Style: In the 1960s, as increasing numbers of women were beginning to develop careers outside the home, they were encouraged to pay attention to the way they spoke in a business environment. In particular they were to avoid asking questions—"Should we consider...?"—in favor of making direct statements. Today that has reversed. The idea is to be less assertive, thereby not so "threatening." Hispanic women especially report having been criticized for being overly expressive. Meanwhile the issue of what is referred to as "locker-room talk" and whether it belongs in the workplace, even when only males are there to hear it, can be distracting, if not outright divisive.

Words and Idioms: Translation from one language to another can be dicey, indeed. For example, the word "kiss" in Swedish means "urine." And LOL in Dutch means "fun." Also, of course, meanings change over time within the same language and within different subcultures. "Bad" is a prime example. In traditional English it's simple—not good. In current colloquial usage, it can mean very good, sexy, etc. On the idiom front, two that might easily come up in a team setting and be confusing to someone newly learning

English are "pitch in" and "going to town." Or consider that the English "pull someone's leg" in Spanish is expressed as *tomar el pelo*—take someone's hair.

Gestures: This is a virtual minefield. There are two that are common and can be lethal. The American "thumb's up" in Nigeria, Australia, Greece or the Middle East essentially is rude and connotes "up yours." The "V for victory" sign has that same crude meaning in South Africa, Australia and the United Kingdom if your palm is facing inward. And, as your mother may well have warned you, pointing can be rude almost anywhere, depending on the context.

For more than a quarter of a century, Roger Axtell's books[2] have been the go-to source for those planning to travel or to do business in cultures with which they are unfamiliar. His work on gestures is a treasure trove of information—and entertainment, in some cases. Several of the stories he relates apply directly to misunderstandings that arise when a gesture means one thing in one country and something entirely different in another. A case in point: when an American firm purchased a German company in the same field, engineers from the two companies began working together. An American engineer suggested a certain "fix" to his German counterpart, who then asked if he were doing it right. The American signaled OK by using his thumb and forefinger to make a circle. The German put down his tools, walked out and refused any more exchange with the American. When a supervisor finally persuaded the two to sit together and reconstruct what happened, he learned that to the German, what the American had signaled was : "You asshole."

Body Language: Casually touching another person is a habit that varies markedly between cultures, both in how often it occurs and how it is interpreted. Man-to-man touching is common in much of the Middle East, Latin America, Russia and Southern Europe. In the US, Japan, Northern Europe and England, it is not, and in America it is sometimes interpreted as an expression of homosexuality. In the wake of the #MeToo Movement, the issue of cross-gender touching calls for careful attention to context and whether or not a touch that is intended to be merely supportive can be misinterpreted. (As this book is being written, the maelstrom created around Joe Biden's habit of touching to offer support is blasting through the media.)

The use of direct eye-contact also varies by culture. In the US and Europe, unless it is sustained and stony, it is considered not only acceptable but a solid show of interest. In many African, Asian and Latin American cultures it can be seen as lack of respect, a challenge of authority or an affront. And, of course, in the Middle East especially among Muslims, direct eye-contact between genders is inappropriate, and when it is practiced by a female may be interpreted to be provocative.

Face-to-face vs. Written, Audio or Video Communication: Predictions vary as to the specific percentage, but there is general agreement among those who study economic trends that the number of people who telecommute is rising exponentially in the U. S. Part of that occurs because technological advances have made it easier and more cost effective, but it also is a result of inclusionary policies by forward-thinking corporations eager to be sensitive to the family needs of their employees. So, it's a good thing, right? Yes, but it requires monitoring and a recognition that even the best video-conferencing falls short of face-to-face exchange when it comes to expressing emotion, communicating nuance and building consensus. A team member watching a video sees what the camera is focused on. If that's not the whole group, it's not the whole story. A text or email exchange is only as good as the communicators are adept in using the medium. Then there is the omnipresent possibility of distractions when team members communicate from remote environments.

Research published in the *Harvard Business Review* in 2012[3] reveals that the most successful teams' communication happens when all team members talk and listen about the same amount of time, face one another, gesture energetically, and connect directly (not just with the team leader) when they're together. It also helps if they carry on side conversations and periodically break, and go out to retrieve pertinent information and bring it back.

MEANT TO MENTOR

A friend of ours began his professional career teaching in a public high school. When he found himself leaving the school most every afternoon a good two hours after the official school day had ended because various students were coming by to talk with him privately, he asked the school guidance counselor if she thought he should perhaps get a degree in counseling. Her answer was quick and insistent. "Absolutely not," she said. "My office is just down the hall from your classroom. I know those students and they know me. I like most of them and I think they like me, but you notice they're not in my office after school. From their point of view, when I listen to them, it's because that's my job. When you do, it's because you care."

Knowing our friend, we would add that his listening skills could have had something to do with what was happening, too, but the point is that same attitudinal variation can be applied to informal mentoring relationships and those that are "official." If the relationship is more assignment than choice, it is the responsibility not just of the mentor, but of the mentee to make an extra effort to ground their work together in trust, and capture the same sense of "helping" that characterizes the mentoring relationships that grow automatically out of mutual trust and admiration.

Be it formal or informal, though, mentoring that works requires clear understandings of its purpose—skills development, how to fit into the organizational culture, increased visibility and likelihood for promotion, etc.—from the get-go. The relationship should feature the complete engagement of both individuals, be methodical but not rigid, and feature agreed-upon ways to measure results. Often, when mentor programs are part of the workplace inclusion initiatives, mentors also act as sponsors or advocates.

> My company would not be where it is today, were it not for the people of integrity who helped me along the way.
>
> ~ Stacey Ferreira | CEO of Forge

On the skills front, there is also a relationship sometimes referred to as "reverse mentoring." A good example is the engagement of a younger, junior associate to train an older manager on how to navigate successfully within a newly developed form of technology. We take issue with the "reverse" descriptor, just as we do with the idea that inclusion presumes the including group is somehow superior to the one being included. (Remember the sandlot basketball team and Kareem we mentioned earlier?) A mentor is a person who has knowledge, experience, wisdom, techniques to share with another; he or she is *not* superior to the other.

When we interviewed Bill Ihrie, former Chief Technology Officer for Intuit, he recalled an excellent example of this sort of mentoring. The company had a policy of hiring 50 to 100 summer interns, whom they sent to the call center for their initial month or six weeks. Because the interns had actually been listening to customer input, they became more conversant with current issues and trends than the full-time project managers. Not only could they inform the process, but they became better prepared to be full-time employees. As Ihrie explained, the purpose of the internship program was to identify and train potential new employees, so the call center experience had multiple paybacks. (See more in the Perspectives section of this chapter.)

That brings up the issue of whether mentoring relationships are stronger if the two people involved share some designation—gender, age, ethnicity. Again, as we discussed earlier, human beings quite naturally feel more comfortable in groups with which they identify. On the other hand, consider the possibility of a more junior member who is one of very few physically disabled individuals on the staff mentoring a senior manager who is a physician in a firm that designs and builds prostheses.

Michele Lee, former Under Secretary of Commerce for Intellectual Property and former Deputy General Counsel at Google (See Perspectives in Chapter 10 for full info.) says that while she recognizes it is appealing to have mentors who "look like you," she counsels young people not to wait for that specific opportunity to arise. "If I had waited for that to happen, I would never have gotten to where I am now," she stresses.

This is perhaps why many firms committed to inclusion build employee resource groups and thereby essentially use homogeneity to accomplish what teams and mentorships use heterogeneity to do. We mentioned McDonalds in the last chapter. Procter and Gamble is an even more aggressive example. On the global level, P&G has organized affinity groups for women leaders, for people with disabilities, and for a gender-group that includes gay, bisexual, lesbian and transgender employees. In the US, there is also a group for veterans and reservists, plus there are leadership teams for those with African ancestry, Asian-Pacific American, Hispanics and Native American Indians.

Tiffany Jana, Founder of TMI Consulting and coauthor of *The B Corporation* Handbook, adds that a strong connection can be formed on the basis of sharing interest or activity in a specific cause. "A values alignment can really give you a head start," she says.

And then on the customer level there are focus groups, measurably enriched if they, too, are inclusive. Not to mention focus groups among employees themselves. As legendary athlete Althea Gibson put it: "No matter what accomplishments you make, somebody helped you."

PERSPECTIVES ON POINT

Insights Gained from Personal Interviews by the Authors

LINDA GRIEGO arguably has as much experience in working with varied groups of people and in public and private organizational settings as one person could fit into a lifetime. Currently an Independent Director of CBS Corp, she has been President and CEO of her own company since 1986, founded and operated a restaurant in downtown Los Angeles, served as Deputy Mayor of Los Angeles, assumed leadership positions in a raft of economic development groups, government commissions and boards of not-for-profit organizations. Then there are the appointments to boards of directors of both publicly traded and private corporations.

Having been reared by her grandmother in a small town in New Mexico, Griego was quick to stress the importance of mentors when she was interviewed in 2017 at an event sponsored by the CBS Diversity Council.[4] Her grandmother, she said, consistently encouraged her, saying: "She who does not look ahead will remain behind." She attributes her own achievements to a combination of luck and a willingness to take risks:

> Yes, I am always inquisitive, eager to learn new things. To me, the hallmark of an entrepreneur is the willingness to act on ideas. But throughout my life, I have had wonderful mentors and sponsors, and I try to be and do the same for

others. I would never close a door behind me. I won't pull you through, but I will make sure the path is open for you to walk through.

In our interview, Griego pointed out vehemently how valuable she considers the writing of Studs Terkel to be. No doubt, she would agree with Terkel when he insists that: "When you become part of something, in some way you count.... To count is very important."

RAVI KURANI probably doesn't spend much time working jigsaw puzzles, but there is little doubt he would be good at it. His skill at seeing where one idea fits with another, one life experience leads to another, one solution can solve multiple problems (fit on all sides) has helped him land a slot on the *Forbes* 2017 list of "30 Under 30" in the energy field. Sutro, Kurani's startup, offers an app/monitor that measures the water quality of pools, warns of problems, and orders supplies, a product born of Kurani's: (1) having learned about pools because of his father's business; (2) having used his Middlebury Institute Frontier Market Scouts assignment in India to study different types of water filters and water cleaning systems; and from that (3) having decided that lots of folks just don't understand water quality.

No doubt based in part on these experiences, Kurani is firm in his conviction that mentoring is not a teacher/student exercise. Yes, on the tactical front, he wants a mentor who has walked the walk, ideally in the same industry he plans to work in. But when they work together, he believes he has a responsibility to return value of some sort. He cites an example. He is in his early 30s; his mentor is in his 60s, and the mentor's father has just died. If Kurani has had an experience with a similar loss, he can offer empathy and support. The relationship is what he calls "bilateral." He also believes that existing bilateral relationships with friends and family can and should serve as a kind of mentorship. As he sees it, one should "build scaffolding that will provide a way to help and be helped, take and give back."

ABHI JHA is Director of Advanced Analytics and Product Management at McKesson, and in that role he mentors a team of data engineers, data scientists, and platform managers focused on product development and deployment. (As a benchmark, McKesson's reported 2018 revenues were $208.4 billion, incorporating pharmaceutical distribution, health information technology, care management tools and medical supplies.) He describes a personal experience early in his career that has convinced him of the value of a strong mentorship relationship.

Struggling with the decision of whether to seek an MBA or not, he contacted a New York University professor who shares Jha's Indian lineage, and had himself earned an MBA at Wharton. "Because of his guidance," Jha remembers, "I was able not only to identify the pros and cons of business school, but also to choose the school best suited for what I wanted [University of Chicago Booth School of Business, where among other activities he served as Co-chair of the Warren Buffett Group]. Making the decision did not end our relationship, though. Every year, we get together and exchange information on how our careers are going and what we are experiencing."

ADELE BURNES not only believes it is possible to make choices that will optimize the value of relationships, be they teams or mentors, but offers a clear list of recommendations on how to do just that. The place to begin, she says, is your employment interview. "Don't work for a company that doesn't fit your values," she insists. And how would you know? "Look at the office when you go to interview...check out the people featured on the leadership page of the website...find what you need in promotional or other materials to scope out where the corporate priorities are." And, she adds, even when you've found a fit, don't stop with the corporate group. "Actively cultivate friendships and seek advice from potential mentors so that you can build your own curated support group outside the corporate setting," she suggests.

If you happen to know Adele herself, you have one good candidate. Her title at YouNoodle is Chief Operating Officer, and a look at her LinkedIn[5] profile reveals that position encompasses a good bit more than you might imagine and that she's pretty happy about it:

> As COO of YouNoodle, I wear many hats; CFO, Head of HR, Captain of Culture, Strategy Lead, Director of Internal Communications, and occasionally Director of Client Happiness and Chief Bottle Washer. I see my role as making sure that everyone in the organization understands the overall vision of the company, understands their role and deliverables towards those goals and is happy and has the resources to be successful. I also make sure all the trains run on time, the bills get paid, and that we continue to grow and sustain ourselves as a company.

> It is a joy to work at a company that is working to level the global playing field for entrepreneurs globally and helping to connect startup with opportunities for growth. We get to work with amazing organizations globally that are hosting startup programs, be it incubators, accelerators, universities, startup prizes, or corporate innovation programs. We provide the software that powers these programs, and the outreach tools to allow organizers to let our community of 200,000+ startups from 180 different countries know about their opportunities for growth.

ARMEN ORUJYAN would qualify, if there were such a word, as the energizer of "entrevation." As Founder and Chairman Emeritus of Athgo he has unleashed an operation that has provided support—financial, intellectual and networking—for nearly 10,000 young entrepreneurs, innovators and students from more than 600 universities in 80 countries. And he has a rather large "footprint" in the public sector, as the Founding Chairman for the Armenian Science & Technology Foundation, a national campaign (including Presidential) guru, a founding member of the UN's Alliance for ICT and Development (GAID), and a member of the Board of Advisors at Rice University's Baker Institute for Public Policy. His affiliations and his achievements are impressive, indeed, but his message is disarmingly simple. Most people, he believes, can and do find coaches and advisors, but few find mentors. How are mentors different? Again, simple, but powerful. "They create an environment where you can feel what you're lacking."

HANA YANG is one of six women who shared their personal stories and professional experiences in a book entitled *Impact with Wings* and cofounded Wingpact, a global angel investment and entrepreneurial community. She argues that there is no "perfect mentor." As she explains it: "You're looking for someone who has empathy for who you are and what you do, not just the same race or gender. I believe we can and should have multiple mentors." She reinforces her support for including various points of view by recalling an experience she had in graduate school at Columbia University: "We were divided into groups and tasked with making a list of what we would take to survive if we were headed to the moon. Our lists were compared to a list created by a group of astronomers, and ours were better. We were not experts, but our perspectives covered more ground." Be it mentors or deciders, inclusion works best!

CRAIG MONTUORI and Jeff Bussgang co-founded Global EIR, a university-based organization formed to help immigrant business founders and their teams create American jobs. Craig had worked as a Caltech rocket engineer, and as the EIR website puts it "decided that fixing problems for startups through the political process was more fun and a bigger set of problems to solve." His take is, no surprise, as informed as it is forthright. As he sees it, immigrant communities tend to be relational rather than transactional, and leaders have a responsibility to not only practice inclusion themselves but make it a foundation from which others will work in the future. He warns against allowing the "status quo" to create and sustain gaps and/or barriers. As an enthusiastic mentor himself, he also insists that the mentoring experience is enriched when the mentees come from different backgrounds, as well as when the mentor learns to "listen and help find solutions, rather than making comments and advising all the time."

EDUARDO PEREZ knows more than a little bit about leading teams. His experience at Visa, where he serves as Senior Vice President and Regional Risk Officer of Visa Latin American and Caribbean, has included (but has not been limited to) driving the adoption of secure digital payment services globally and throughout Latin America and the Caribbean. He emphasizes that promoting diversity and inclusion is not only the right thing to do, it is the profitable thing for companies to do. Several empirical studies indicate that more diverse and inclusive companies produce higher earnings and better stock price performance over time. In 2015, Perez was one of three Visa employees interviewed as part of Hispanic Heritage Month. He noted that he had learned how much individual access is dependent on others, and as a result has a habit of following three principles: ask for help, help others whenever you can, and never count yourself out. He added that Hispanic Heritage month offers the opportunity to celebrate all of the "diverse cultures and countries that the Hispanic community represents and all of the valuable contributions they have made to advance the United States. It is also a great time to be proud to be an American."[6]

KENYA WILEY served as Counsel and Senior Policy Advisor for the US Senate Committee on Homeland Security and Governmental Affairs before joining the legal department of the Motion Picture Association of America (MPAA). She then founded Fashion Innovation Alliance, where she uses her expertise in law, public policy, social justice and specifically diversity and inclusion issues to advise and help build community for companies in fashion, technology and retail. Within each of the economic sectors in which she's worked, she has seen leaders search for tangible steps to take to institutionalize inclusiveness. She agrees that mentoring is key, and also stresses that hiring is not enough. "If the folks you hire are all slotted into entry-level positions, you have not succeeded in creating an inclusive operation," she explains. "Also, in addition to formal mentoring, it is crucial to assure that small-scale personal relationships—a cup of coffee in the morning, a backyard barbecue, a round of golf—are developed with people. That's mentoring, too, and it matters."

ERNESTINE FU would drive those people who insist that the analytic mind and the artistic mind don't co-exist in one person crazy. As a venture partner at Alsop Louie Partners since 2011 (when she was still in school), she has taken the lead with companies involved in disruptive technologies, while at the same time advising startups outside the firm in a full range of activities, including such things as gaming and mobile analytics. That's not all. She founded a not-for-profit organization of her own while she was still a teen. She co-authored Civic Work, Civic Lessons, a book on philanthropy, with Stanford Law School Dean Tom Ehrlich, and the two of them wrote for *Forbes* magazine. She believes passionately that young people need to use technology to become engaged in civic endeavors.

With widely different backgrounds and several decades difference in age, the two authors are quick to report that their venture provided a learning experience for both. Prior to meeting Ehrlich, Fu had no firsthand experience with what she terms "what exactly it means to devote a career to public service." As she describes their relationship, he was in the beginning an inspirational role model; and then became a mentor, colleague and friend. For his part, Ehrlich points out that while he had known that young people were engaged in civic work, it was only after he met Fu that he realized "how committed young people are, making amazing differences in the lives of those around them."[7]

In *Civic Work, Civic Lessons*[8] Fu recalls a high school music teacher, Chris Rodriguez, whose tirelessness and dedication made an event for homeless children possible. And she adds: "Mr. Rodriguez was more than just a sounding board, or someone who provided a fresh perspective, as many mentors do; he was able to support me, yet let me fall, recognize achievements yet challenge me, and in the process gain my trust."

While he did not carry the title of "mentor," she told us in our interview, he was the perfect example of what it means—"Show Up, Set Up, Help, Support."

MARTY HU doesn't hesitate when you ask him what effect mentoring can have. A Co-founder and currently CTO of Prodigy, a provider of software for the automotive retail industry, Hu is pretty certain he would not have gone the entrepreneurial route if it weren't for a professor at Stanford University. It was his freshman year, and when the professor suggested the project he had submitted might be good enough to be the basis for a startup, he was on his way. The two worked together over the summer and became friends, and eventually the professor invested in what Hu was putting together. With his earlier company having been acquired by Dropbox, Hu and Michia Rohrssen founded Prodigy in 2015. It is on its way to $10 billion in car sales per year. The two men were named to the *Forbes* 30 Under 30 List and are now on the speakers' circuit sharing their enthusiasm about business and science.

BRIAN RASHID is a storyteller. Yep, really. Maybe you won't be so difficult to convince when you learn the name of his business is *A Life in Shorts*. His clients span the globe, he travels between New York and Colombia, and the services he provides have to do with—wait for it—branding, monetizing your message, and brand strategy. When he considers the idea of mentoring, he gets the impression that lots of folks have things upside down. With or without actually labeling the process "mentoring," he argues that the entry question should be "What can I do for you?" not vice versa. Why? Because in most cases there is something you can give in return, even if it's just filling out a foursome for golf. What's more, he stresses, people are sensitive to being "used," so forming a friendship works better all around. From that, it's possible to build an actual community or a team, friends of course, but clients, too. Finally, Rashid insists that the best mentor of all is not actually a human being or a relationship, but experience itself, if you take action based on that experience. "We learn," he sums it up, "when we TRY IT."

DANIELLE STRACHMAN is all about education—what it means, how it should be designed to work best, what part is institutional and what part is experiential. In some ways, she not only "thinks outside the box," but tries her hand at redesigning the box itself. She founded a K-8 charter school, worked with Peter Thiel on his out-of-the-classroom-into-the-business-builder scholarship initiative, and currently serves as general partner of 1517, a venture capital fund she cofounded. The fund's intended clients are business founders who are high school and college age, know the value of teamwork and aren't afraid of edgy ideas. "Knowledge and practice," she says, "are two different skill sets." So far as mentorship goes, she sees some downsides in limiting oneself to a formal mentor/mentee relationship, or even in defining a relationship that already is supportive that way. "By making it formal," she points out, "you can take away some of its value." Even more important than one-on-one relationships are "communities that you can and should build around yourself and your work." That, of course, is fertile ground for inclusion, and for extension. "When I am able to get a group of good people in a room together," Strachman elaborates, "I begin to see them as accelerators of other people. Each goes out into his own community and ideas spread."

JULIA JAYNE, President of the Jayne Law Group, has been teaching at UC Hastings College of Law for nearly two decades, in addition to practicing law. As we discuss the mentoring process, she notes that when she decided to establish her own practice she had experience only in the practice of law (as a member of another firm), not in the entrepreneurial area, so essentially "flew solo." In the years since, she has focused on networking, on establishing a reputation that will engender referrals from other attorneys, and on taking indigent cases. Aware that she is now in a position to be helpful to others, as well as to use her practical experience in the classroom, she offers support where she can, but somewhat apologetically—and in our opinion incorrectly—does not describe herself as a "mentor." Hers is an excellent example of building, as Strachman in the interview above recommends, a "community."

KAIA SIMMONS was enrolled in Harvard Business School when we held our interview. She had already earned both undergraduate and Master of Science degrees at Stanford University, after which she spent three years at the Stripes Group, a New York City based venture capital firm. She is quick to say that on multiple occasions she has been the beneficiary of mentorship. "I never really sought it out," she explains. "It sort of happened 'organically,' and to me that made it seem especially authentic." A competitive swimmer, she had initially been mentored in high school by her coach. Then while she was still at Stanford, she consulted a partner in the venture capital firm where she worked about whether he considered business school a real plus. "He talked a good deal about the human side of the experience," she remembers, "and not only was he right, it was a big help." And then she added, "I was really blessed at Stripes Group. My boss, Karen, is a mom with two kids, the only female partner at the time, and she graciously guided me through not just professional issues, but life things: relationships, dating, should I really go to business school now that I've been accepted. She was wonderful, and it was possible because the culture of the firm was open, which made it quite different from other private equity firms in New York."

KEN KANNAPPAN, former CEO of Plantronics, would and did in our interview strongly support Simmons' point about the strength of "organic mentoring." Once his company had achieved a level of inclusion that they were working toward (and one well above average) he tried to "force mentoring," as he calls it. "It worked relatively poorly," he recalls. "What works is to create a natural, fertile environment, and let them mentor on their own. I would advise against even encouraging, but do reward." (See more about Kannappan's experience in the next chapter.)

FEBIN BELLAMY, one of the youngest, if not *the* youngest individual we interviewed for this book, must have had a distinct feeling of *déjà vu* when he graduated from Georgetown University and received the Undergraduate Dean's Award as the one graduating student who had made the most notable contribution in the area of social entrepreneurship. That was the fourth such honor. He was also named 2017 Student Entrepreneur of the Year and received the Lena Landegger Award, the university's most distinguished community service award for undergraduate students. Yes, you're right, that's just three. But he had also received the President's Award for Leadership at Rockland Community College when he graduated in 2014.

Bellamy is Founder and CEO of Unsung Heroes Media, a company he started while he was still a student to recognize the contributions of people working in high school and college settings who might otherwise go unnoticed. The company has been featured by the likes of *Forbes*, BBC, and *USA Today*. Bellamy is quick to say most all of what he has been able to do has been made possible by mentors. "These people opened all kinds of doors," he remembers. "They made calls to the media, they found donors and donated themselves, amazing stuff." To what does he attribute that kind of support? "To me, if you want help, you must be up front about what you need," he insists. "It is important to be honest about who you are and where you came from, to be scrappy, to be authentic. I can't remember who said it, but I believe whoever it was who said, 'If you want to go fast, go by yourself. If you want to go far, you need other people.'"

TERESA BRIGGS spent her 37 year career at Deloitte LLP where she was a member of the Deloitte board of directors and previously served the firm in a variety of positions, most recently Managing Partner first in the Silicon Valley office, then in the same role in San Francisco and finally in the Western Region. She is currently a member of the board of directors of ServiceNow (NYSE: NOW) and Warby Parker. Throughout her professional career she has taken leadership roles in community organizations, and she believes strongly in the impact that corporations can and should make by being socially conscious.

As we discuss the role of personal relationships in a business setting, she focuses on the difference between mentors and sponsors. She explains:

> A mentor provides coaching, career advice, and is someone you consider a role model in your workplace. A sponsor goes much further. Generally, the sponsor is at least two levels above you in the organization and, because of that, has a line of sight that you don't have. He (In my case, my sponsor was a man) put his personal capital on the line to help me spot and land opportunities, offered feedback at critical moments, etc. In return, since he went out on a limb for me, I felt a deep responsibility to deliver for him. For me that meant I did my best work, but also had the most fun. My sponsor gave me lots of responsibility, and never micromanaged, but if he saw something he thought was problematic, he had no problem diving in to help. And as my skills grew, he migrated to the role of leading a leader.

As her career developed, Briggs realized she had learned not only the requisite skills, but her own style of leadership from her sponsor. And then, after she turned 50, with the realization that she was only a dozen years from the Deloitte mandatory retirement age, she became an active sponsor in her own right. When she began to look for the best partner to whom to transition her premium client, "one of the younger partners with whom I worked was, interestingly enough, my former sponsor's son. Like his father he is super talented, and when it turned out that I was able to transition my client to him, it felt as if I had completed the circle of life."

NADIA YAKOOB is quick to point out that she has been the beneficiary of mentoring denies any suggestion of hierarchy or power-posturing. Her decision to become an immigration attorney was not merely informed but essentially defined by law school professors. Having served as a legal intern for the UN High Commission on Refugees, she realized that working on refugee and immigration issues was what she found fulfilling, and struggled with how she would repay student loans if she chose to continue with a not-for-profit organization. "It was my professors who convinced me to investigate firms that specialize in immigration law," she remembers. Now managing attorney of her own firm in Oakland, CA, she candidly admits that her relationship with interns and paralegal employees is definitely a form of "lateral mentoring." She says:

> I truly wouldn't be as up-to-date on technology if it weren't for the Millennials who come here and end up teaching me. What's more, I have learned from them that it's possible to discover how to do, find, learn lots and lots of things just by an adept Google search or YouTube offering. And it's been exciting for me to see them use their time in this small firm environment to launch their careers in some of the most prestigious large firms.

Each one teach one!

JESSICA MAH is a big fan of peer groups and believes they are often more powerful than mentorship arrangements. Founder and CEO of InDinero, a company designed to help entrepreneurs run better businesses that appeared among *Inc.* magazine's list of the fastest growing companies in America, Mah describes the mentor relationship as too often being subject to what she calls a "wild power dynamic." It is easy to discern that in the almost ten years that she has been part of InDinero, she has seen the full array of cultural, personal, and emotional forces that can define the workplace. "Working out the practical is actually pretty easy," she notes. "The psychological can be another thing altogether." In terms of inclusion, for example, she defines the issue simply: "everyone, yes *everyone* has to have a voice." Then with trademark candor she adds, "When you do that right, and listen to all points of view working toward some kind of consensus, you by necessity slow things down. It's important to recognize and acknowledge that up front."

JENNIFER LEHMANN WENG is Executive Director of the Chief Executives Organization, an exclusive global organization for distinguished leaders of the Young Presidents' Organization. As a YPO member herself, she notes that the organization's Forums are often defined as "your own personal board of directors" and incorporate in regular monthly meetings as well as annual retreats the kind of information sharing that allows each participant to benefit from the experience of his/her peers. "I remember one retreat where we developed and presented a 'lifeline'. The feeling of vulnerability and trust that created set the stage for a real peer-based exchange of perspectives."

STEPHANIE MCGANN JANTZEN knows what it's like to deal with the tough issues in the tough spotlight's-on-you-watch-out situations. Currently, she is Vice President at Perry Communications Group (PCG), a firm that is recognized for work in issues management and public affairs. She has worked in a Presidential campaign, managed various statewide and local campaigns, served for more than a dozen years as Chief of Staff in the office of a local politician, staffed political conventions, acted as the advance lead for former Presidents as well as local politicians, and been California consultant to the World Trade Center. And that's just the public side. In the corporate arena, she worked with two tech start-ups and served as interim CEO for an established tech company, not to mention public relations and political strategy consulting.

Because of her acumen and her reputation, McGann Jantzen receives multiple requests daily for interviews, so we begin ours by being completely candid and asking just exactly why she has agreed to speak with us. "It's the title of your proposed book," she responds, just as candidly. "Yes, there is a different way to do different. I like people who want to create a more understanding, compassionate and innovative world, and have enough hope to believe that's possible. And I also admire those who recognize that there are barriers to overcome and talk about how to do it."

She ends up spending nearly an hour with us, an hour punctuated with laughs, which is her trademark, and with thoughtful, practical perspectives, such as (abbreviated here):

> *What is the role of technology in the future?* Technology is the window into opportunity. Lack of technology is one way we destroy any hope of a level playing field.

> *How does policy fuel innovation?* There are lots of ways to approach this, but an important one is social justice. Whether they're on the local, state or federal level, policies that fundamentally encourage inclusion can matter.

Consider access to higher education, again part of the level playing field. There are brilliant young kids living in deeply impoverished communities who need to (1) believe they can participate; (2) know that there are people around who want to inspire them; and (3) offered education that isn't limited to subjects like how to balance a checkbook. They could be real players in all kinds of ways. We need to look at the policies, and see whom they help and whom they don't help.

How are we doing on inclusion? We just are not there yet when it comes to inclusion. I talked with one tech CEO who said if he wanted to really build something new and exciting, he would hire a global team of all females. Also, we need to change the narrative about immigrants. We are all human, and we all have something to bring to the table. There is never only one solution to any problem. If everyone in on the decision is exactly the same, they may not even be conscious that they're missing something. And in the US, we are hopelessly title-driven. Just because someone is working as a receptionist does not mean that his or her perspective has no merit.

Move over world, here we come!

ENDNOTES

[1] https://ecorner.stanford.edu/article/tip-your-hat-to-your-team/.

[2] Roger Axtell, "Gestures: The Do's and Taboos of Body Language Around the World," https://www.scribd.com/document/157812654/Gestures-the-Do-s-and-Taboos-of-Body-La-Axtell-Roger-E-Print.

[3] hbr.org/2012/04/the-new-science-of-building-great-teams.

[4] (https://www.cbscorporation.com/wp-content/uploads/2018/04/10.25.17.pdf).

[5] https://www.linkedin.com/in/adeleburnes/.

[6] http://visacorporate.tumblr.com/post/131225143593/visas-voices-honoring-hispanic-heritage-month.

[7] https://www.kettering.org/sites/default/files/periodical-article/HEX-2013-Fu-Ehrlich.pdf.

[8] Thomas Erlich and Ernestine Fu. "Civic Work, Civic Lessons: Two Generations Reflect on Public Service," https://books.google.com/books?id=xWUSAAAAQBAJ&pg=PA67&lpg=PA67&d-q=civic+work+civic+lessons+mentorship&source=bl&ots=jq3zC0298P&sig=ACfU3U0hp-wi6kPxrh4nd5kbxchulv6kovg&hl=en&sa=X&ved=2ahUKEwi676vT9MvhAhWs1lkKHXJ2Ay-QQ6AEwBnoECAkQAQ#v=onepage&q=%20mentor&f=false.

CHAPTER TEN

What's Next?

———

At the end of 2018 the UK's *Guardian* newspaper, a welcome source for people who like their news to be reliable, but not redundant, asked four different individuals considered experts in their respective fields to describe what life on earth will be like in 2050.[1]

Theoretical physicist Michio Kaku focused on telepathic communication and medical advances that will not only increase human longevity, but reduce the ravages of aging to the point that the longer life is also a longer youth.

Astrophysicist Neil deGrasse Tyson predictably dealt with space as not merely a tourist attraction but a site for global commerce.

Futurist Faith Popcorn, the Founder and CEO of BrainReserve, wrote about the advances of artificial intelligence on the health front, including psychology. She also addressed gender fluidity, noting that Facebook has identified 71 kinds of gender, and that nearly half the Millennials see gender as a spectrum. There will be, she predicted, no pattern, wherein one gender takes care of another or bosses it around. More than 30 years ago, she had predicted the melding of races, so that everyone would be "brown," and she stills sees racial distinctions dying. What will not disappear, though, according to her theory, are differences in intelligence, based not on native intelligence, but on having the money to take advantage of AI or to purchase intelligence-enhancing drugs. The result she says will be people with and people without, unless some social class intervenes to save those without.

And finally, Amy Zalman, Founder of the Strategic Narrative Institute, addressed what kinds of jobs will be affected by automation. As she put it: "It's not that automation will change work. It's that work will change so drastically that we'll need to give what we do a different name."

If automation causes significant displacement, she believes human ingenuity will step in to revise social services systems, send people back to school, create new kinds of work. Wealth inequality, as it has in the past, will continue to provide access for some classes to get a better education, but also since they will be able to afford it, they also will be able to take advantage of biological and genetic enhancements born of medical advances.

As we mentioned briefly in Chapter 8, those of us in positions of leadership today can, with collaborative decision-making that harnesses ideas and initiatives from multiple perspectives, have a material affect on the future. That means using inclusion now to diminish exclusion 50 years from now and in the meantime building businesses that will be set to grow from automation, not be killed by it.

That sounds a little lofty, but the opportunity is real. And, for you, does it gain in immediacy at all if you recognize that some of the jobs that are predicted to disappear are those of attorneys and accountants, jurists and journalists? Yes, entry-level, unskilled positions are the primary target, but not the only one. According to a Brookings Institution study[2] those with less than a Bachelor's Degree face a 55 percent risk, but those with a Bachelor's Degree face a 24 percent risk—they are not exempt.

If you know someone who recognizes the problem, but denies that any of the burden of responsibility falls to the business sector, ask that person three questions:

1. Is it better to create a society where most people have jobs and thereby buying power or to tax the wealthy individuals and successful corporations to provide public programs to protect people whose skills are no longer in demand?

2. Where is the power to effect change? Did you know that 69 of the world's 100 largest economic entities are corporations, and the other 31 are countries?[3]
3. If your employees and your customers are better educated, does that help or harm your business?

What, then, can business leaders do to prepare for imminent change, and turn it from threat to opportunity? Since you're reading this book, there is a chance you're already engaged. If not—or if you'd like to do more—take at look at our Three-by-Three Strategy/Task Matrix.

STRATEGY:

Educate Our Existing Employees So They Will Be Skill-Ready for Changes in Job Requirements

Three Tasks

1. Form partnerships with colleges to solve the affordability issues surrounding higher education via tuition assistance programs or skill-based programs like coding boot camps a la the Starbucks/Arizona State University program.[4]
2. Remember that managers and C-suite types are employees, too, and engage the power of mentorship that goes in both directions. Edelman, the world's largest independent PR firm, has a program it has named "Rotnem," (mentor spelled backward) through which the mentee is the senior employee.[4] This is an especially efficient way to narrow the gap regarding knowledge of and comfort with technology.

3. Use affinity groups (also sometimes referred to as employee resource groups) to monitor how "included" their colleagues actually feel, to speak up when necessary, and to call for change when it's needed. Nothing is more crucial to business success than hiring the right people—except keeping them. Employees who feel valued are eager to learn, more able to advance, and far more likely to meet change with "Of course, I would like to learn to do that. When do we start?"

STRATEGY:

Build Trust in Our Company So That It
Can Weather Economic and Social Change

Three Tasks

1. It can be argued that building trust requires different approaches for different stakeholders. We would instead argue that the basic elements are the same; it is the level of emphasis or perhaps the focus that changes. Ethical business practices, transparency and accountability are the core, be it for investors, government regulators, clients, board members, vendors or employees. Yes, the OSHA inspector and the security guard in the foyer will use different measures, in fact they will be aware of different things. But both will feel betrayed and respond negatively if you don't "walk the walk." So what is the task? Anilu Vazquez-Ubarri, Chief Human Resources Officer at TPG Global, speaking specifically about the issue of inclusion[4] notes that often people see the task as trying to "boil the ocean." It is,

instead, she suggests, a matter of everyone—not just the person whose assignment it is, not just the person who's in charge—doing the ordinary things, every day, all the time. Create a culture where that happens. How? Building and supporting employee alliance groups; becoming involved in local community programs and organizations; letting vendors know you expect certain practices on their part; calling the board's attention to what you are doing, not just to keep them informed, but to get their buy-in and ideally their participation.

2. Trust is also inexorably connected to the social and cultural values of the location in which you are doing business and the values of the people who live and work there. Be aware of the words, images and gestures that transmit different ideas in different places. We talked in Chapter 9 about the "thumb's up" gesture, and how in some places it's considered not just rude, but crude. We've seen it in large form on Google advertising, and there it sits as the "Like" symbol on Facebook. Does that matter in other countries, or in the US for people from other countries? Replace the thumb with the middle finger in those places, and see how you react. Are there similar instances in anything your company communicates? Find out and change what you need to.

3. Just as customers and potential employees find it easier to trust companies that promote policies of equity, inclusion, and transparency, they turn away from those they believe do not do that. Lots of research points to how destructive unconscious bias can be. Guard against that by using algorithms or the consulting firms that provide them to detect potential problems in language or images; take names off job applications and resumes when they're being evaluated and do the same for customer complaints; do whatever it takes to make face-to-face exchanges, be they with

employees, customers, applicants, vendors or investors, comfortable for all parties, open, honest and informative *beyond what is expected.*

STRATEGY:

Stay on Top of Innovation to Harness the Power of Technology and Lead Instead of React

Three Tasks

1. Remember that an inclusive operation is, by definition, more innovative. Why? The greater the difference between people working together to solve a problem or create a product the larger the number of ideas presented. And if that group is working in a truly inclusive environment, meaning that everyone feels comfortable presenting her/his ideas, the number of ideas can be exponentially increased. It is important to assemble relevant data, too. As one example, a 2018 study[5] investigating the effect of gender diversity on boards in STEM&F sectors found that at least 30 percent of women is important. A number lower than that can result in the creation of subgroups, conflicts, and lack of trust.

2. Analyze demographic and other trends at least 10 years out, and use the findings to inform strategic planning. A case in point for the retail segment is a study published by Canvas8[6] that defines six global trends for 2019:

    a. Inclusion and diversity in beauty with brands targeted to the full range of genders, sexual preferences and skin color, plus increased use of technology with machines that generate single applications of beauty products.

b. Greater emphasis on responsible consumerism, to include not only environmental concerns but careful evaluation of information and the sources from which it comes.

c. More attention to healthy eating, not only in choosing food, but supporting local agriculture.

d. Taking advantage of various technological solutions to create a safe and healthy home environment.

e. A desire for luxury items from the wealthiest, best educated and most connected of millennials.

f. A convergence of digital and physical shopping, e.g., sales personnel in brick and mortar settings using AI.

3. Innovation is not limited to new products and processes. Indeed, the potential for greatest change may well arise from effective collaborations and different applications of existing products and systems. For example, in 2017 the BBC published a list of *ideas* that are set to change the world. Included were:

a. A character (think Muppet) has been created to teach the 2.5 billion people in the world without toilets how to use them.

b. Six EU countries participated in an effort to use cloned moss to monitor air pollution.

c. Google Earth worked with Brazil's indigenous people to pinpoint destruction of the rainforest.

d. Indonesia allows citizens to trade trash for access to health care.

Yes, these are all related to environmental issues. But then, environmental issues are global, so that says something about the value of replication.

Dean Kamen, inventor of the Segway, says it well: "Every once in a while, a new technology, an old problem and a big idea turn into an innovation."[7]

Be sure your team captures those.

Perhaps at no time in the history of the United States has there been a greater need for corporate leaders with access to sufficient funding, appropriate technology (that keeps changing to remain appropriate) and employees on all organizational levels to whom they listen and from whom they reap ideas to step up.

PERSPECTIVES ON POINT

Insights Gained from Personal Interviews by the Authors

STEVE ST. ANGELO was only two days into retirement when we caught up with him for our interview. He had spent more than four decades in the automotive industry, having most recently served as CEO and Senior Manager for Latin America and the Caribbean Region at Toyota. Perhaps not surprisingly, since he is trained in kaizen (sometimes spelled kaisen), the Japanese philosophy of continuous improvement, he immediately addressed the changes that are likely within the next decade. (The literal English translation of kaizen is "good change.") Toyota, he points out, is already working on a device that will make it possible for those who have never been able to walk to do just that. He hastens to add that expected improvements are by no means limited to products, but will also arise in manufacturing processes and the ways and speed with which service is provided.

St. Angelo's professional experience includes more than one instance when that kind of change has happened. In 2017, for example, the Toyota Production System team provided support for trainers at Santa Cruz Hospital in São Paulo, Brazil. It produced a 30-minute reduction in wait time for the hospital's patients.

STEVE WESTLY brings to the issue of inclusion a wealth of experience in the public, private and not-for-profit sectors. He served as State Controller of California before becoming one of the leading candidates in the Democratic primary for Governor of California in 2006, and was California Co-chair for Obama for America two years later. On the private side of the ledger, he has had leadership experience in technology, investment banking, and higher education. Currently he is Founder and Managing Partner of The Westly Group, one of the country's larger sustainability venture firms, and he and his wife also operate the Westly Foundation, which provides health care and education services for children and underserved communities throughout their home state. With an eye specifically to the work of the Foundation, we asked Westly what he thought would be the most effective pro-active steps a business leader might take, especially in more rural communities. His answer addressed not only the local issues, but a more global perspective. As he sees it, rare is the company that does not wish to expand internationally. What is important is to make sure managers, especially those in charge of hiring, realize that inclusion is a crucial element in the ability to do that successfully. Since he is also has served on the board of Tesla, there's an excellent chance he has witnessed firsthand just what happens when a manufacturing operation strikes a balance between developing cutting edge technology and finding the way to sell it across the cultural and economic levels of societies the world over.

MARGARET NEALE has contributed in multiple ways to the understanding of organizational behavior, with special focus on negotiation, team-building and inclusion. (Indeed, as this book is being written, the Stanford Graduate School of Business is planning a two-day event to honor her work.) She gives new—and quite practical—definition to the phrase "win-win." We say "practical," because she advises not only an attitude that works well, but specific, tangible, recognizable, *learnable* steps. In our interview, we heard two perspectives that speak directly to business leaders interested in building inclusionary practices not only in the private sector, but within the social order. Regarding inclusion, she said: "One of the benefits of networks is that they give you access to information that you wouldn't normally have." And then as to motivation, she is insistent: "Good intentions are great, but they are not sufficient. You also have to have clear goals, and managers have to be held accountable."

SHERRI HALLORAN has had a front row seat to watch how the issue of inclusion plays out not only in the corporate world, but also among the leaders of not-for-profit organizations and those focused on science education. Having started her professional career working with staffing and training issues, she spent six years as Field Marketing Manager for Red Bull before moving to the Virginia Biotechnology Association in 2008. In her role as Vice President for Membership and Programs, she works not only with the association's members but also holds leadership positions with the state organization for those who serve in managerial roles for professional and trade associations. She sees inclusion as "an area that industry as a whole, nationwide, is focused on," as well as "an ongoing conversation...a scenario that has to evolve and grow and change."

GREG BECKER (See more complete professional info in the Perspectives listing for Chapter 7.) sees an inclusionary culture as crucial to a business person's ability to think beyond the norm in not only starting a business set to succeed but also keeping it on that track. Having worked more than a quarter of a century at Silicon Valley Bank, where a good bit of the focus is on fast-growing companies in the technology sector, he has witnessed how inclusion lays the groundwork for "not thinking about things the standard way and challenging each other." He explains further: "It truly comes from having a diverse group of founders and a diverse group of people to start the company." He also is an active supporter of community involvement, on the part of the bank and of its employees. When SVB won the Best Buddies Employer of the Year Award in 2016, he pointed out that since Best Buddies is an organization devoted to helping people (many of them young adults) with intellectual disabilities be trained, get jobs and find friendships, the award "means we're helping those individuals accomplish what they want to accomplish."[8]

FELIPE CHÁVEZ CORTÉS is CEO and Co-founder of Kiwi Campus, a firm that employs robots for food delivery. The company began its service on the UC Berkley campus, and is expanding from there. One of his team's first discoveries was that the system is significantly reducing the times food delivery takes as well as the attendant costs. The number of robots in service has grown rapidly, and the Kiwi Campus team has designed a system that relies on, yes, a TEAM of robots, some assigned to take food from restaurants, and some tasked with delivery from the vehicle to the customer. Early operations were in the San Francisco Bay area and Colombia. So, a new group to include! Chávez told us he believes "there is one characteristic that all successful CEOs in the world have, and that is that they never give up. I think that is much easier when you have a good team."

DAVID HORNIK likes ideas—those who have them, those who disrupt them, those who share them, and those who drop them for better ones. He's done a rather thorough job of setting up a variety of environments in and through which to stimulate idea generation. He teaches at both Harvard Law School and the Stanford Graduate School of Business (Maybe he also likes airplane interiors?), has served for almost two decades as General

Partner at August Capital, an early stage high tech venture investor, and founded The Lobby Conference in 2007. Since he hasn't really enough to do, he is also the Executive Producer there, building dates, times and arenas for lively gatherings of idea mongers and their cohorts. Not surprisingly, Hornik agrees heartily with all the statistics that argue inclusion is a cornerstone of success. But he warns that unless those in leadership positions are intentional about making it happen, it is not likely to. "We have to specifically encourage all kinds of folks to pitch their businesses to us."

And how would he suggest an investor do that? "I serve on the board of directors of GLAAD, the organization dedicated to building acceptance for the LGBT community," David explains. "I hope that in doing so I am being clear about being accepting and about taking action not just for that community, but for any other marginalized groups."

ERIC SCHMIDT, widely recognized for his tenure as CEO of Google, remains on the board of directors of Alphabet, the holding company. He may well be one of the most quoted American CEOs of the 21st century. (One of our favorites is: "Fast learners win.") In our interview, he is quite careful not to "speak for Google," but he is informed and articulate about future trends in US industry and how they are affected by corporate leadership's learning to embrace inclusion as a core value and a working model. And there is improvement in the "pipeline" for some segments of the economy. Schmidt cited, for example, medicine, a point supported by the fact that 2017 marked the first year in US history that women outranked men in the number enrolled in medical school.

At the same time, Schmidt is the first to agree that the problem is not solved—instead it is "in the process of being solved." To explain, he adds: "There is a great deal of research revealing that if ability is broadly diffuse because people with different backgrounds are involved, businesses flourish…. So far as products go, what I mean is you get a better product, not necessarily a different product, as in one built, say, for women." To make greater strides toward even more progress, he suggests that the society at large should take steps to close the gaps created, be it by poverty, direct or indirect discrimination, or lack of access to education.

KEN KANNAPPAN retired as CEO of Plantronics in August of 2016, and almost exactly a year later was appointed Chairman of Integrated Device Technology. He remembers: "At Plantronics, we tried to create a really good workplace, so we could keep our talent. The 'bad news' is it worked. We had incredibly high retention, which meant that our people were far older than the rest of the workforce in Silicon Valley." When the leaders looked at market statistics, they realized the buyers of their products were increasingly those over 30. Their core market, office professionals on the phone two hours or more per day, were mostly Millennials who preferred the products of their competitors. "Our people, naturally, had an implicit bias toward creating products that they wanted. When we tried to hire Millennials, we found we had a number of handicaps. We'd have a company party. Our longtime employees arrived round 6, had drinks and dinner, danced a bit and left at 10. The Millennials arrived at 9 or 10, planning to leave at 3. We had not been thinking up front of how holistically to solve the problem."

Kannapan believes a similar issue could occur with different ethnicities. "We had a strict rule in every country in which we operated to only hire local people. We soon decided we needed to have some people from those countries in our headquarters office, too. The deal is to match your operations to the demographics you're trying to win. Or, put simply, do what fits your business."

PAUL BRADLEY (See career details in the Perspectives section of Chapter 8.) has been on a unique global career path, working across various industries (including government, supply chain management, creating new ventures, etc.) and spanning leadership roles across 14 different countries. This has formed for him a worldview that incorporates embracing change and thriving on working with people from different cultures. Statistics puncuate his description:

- Asia is vibrant, dynamic and home to 2/3 of the world's population.
- ASEAN member nations are home to more than 622 million people, with a large youth demographic.
- Singapore has a population of 5.6 million, and one of the highest national reserves (top 10) of any country in the world.
- Singapore has a 91 percent home ownership rate, the highest in the world.
- By 2025, more than 50,000 warehouses will be robotic.

To deal with the trends that can be expected to emerge from numbers such as these, Bradley insists corporate leaders must redesign their organizations, making them ready for not only technological, but also environmental and political disruptions. The way to do that, he insists, is to include in strategy and operations a multiplicity of cultures and perspectives, leveraging from that mix to create a business that is both "cohesive and dynamically adaptable."

TIFFANY JANA does just about everything one could do to promote inclusion. As Founder of TMI Consulting Inc., she teaches it, nurtures it, strategizes with a wide range of clients on how to achieve it. She speaks about it (and also about maximizing human potential and building extraordinary workplaces). She writes about it, as in books, three of them so far. One of those books is about B Corporations, and Jana talks about that subject in our discussion.

> There is no crystal ball, but it is important to emphasize inclusion and put measurable energy behind it. As part of the B Corporation Movement, people are beginning to recognize the power we have to shape our future, to create the world we want to see when we make ourselves and our institutions accountable, and consider ourselves citizens of the world. By rewarding B Corporations with our votes, our dollars and our praise, the number of people engaged will increase and the effect on profit margins will be enormous.

The B Corporation Handbook, which Jana co-authored with Ryan Honeyman, is in its second edition, revised in part to put a stronger focus on what the authors call "DEI" or diversity, equity and inclusion. They spoke with more than 200 B Corps across the globe to discover how they are improving their environmental and social performance as well as working to build a more inclusive economy.

ALAINA PERCIVAL, CEO of Women Who Code (See detailed information in Perspectives section of Chapter 4.), is bullish on the trajectory of change that is now possible for women. "When my mother graduated from college, she believed she had three career choices: nurse, secretary or teacher," Percival explains. "We're still working on the mind shift, but the idea is to see women choosing as goals such roles as doctor, engineer, venture capitalist, head of department. The more women we see excelling in such roles, the more we will be inspired to pursue them. And focusing on the technology sector is especially wise because every industry will eventually have a tech component."

MARTINA WELKHOFF is already living in a world that many of us cannot even describe. As founding partner of the WXR Venture Fund she has not only defined, but jumped feet first into the nexus between the latest shift in technology and the contributions of women to that shift. "In the end," she explains, "what we are essentially doing is providing a platform to showcase the leadership of women contributing to the next computing paradigm." A quick look at some of the companies in the 2018 WXR cohort reveals innovative products in education, health care, e-commerce and more. As Welkhoff told us, "What we hope to do is normalize the idea of women in leadership, so that the focus is on their work instead of on their being women." As advisor to the Center for Leadership and Strategic Thinking at the University of Washington and a World Economic Forum Global Shaper, Welkhoff isn't new to this "game," and her talent and experience are no doubt as important to the women whom she's supporting as is the funding she's helping develop.

MICHELLE LEE describes her career as "starting out in tech, then law, then the corporate world at Google, and most recently government at the U.S. Patent and Trademark office. That's correct, but also minimal. She has been a visiting professor at Stanford University (from which she also earned her Law Degree), serves on the Advisory Council for the MIT Media Lab (holding both Bachelors and Masters Degrees in electrical engineering and computer science from MIT), was Deputy General Counsel at Google during its formative years, and spent 3.5 years as the CEO of the U.S. Patent and Trademark Office, one of the largest intellectual property offices in the world with 13,000 employees and an annual budget of $3.4 billion. She is also the first woman and person of color to hold this position (as the Under Secretary of Commerce and Director of the U.S. Patent and Trademark Office) in our country's history. In 2005, she and six other women founded ChIPs, a not-for-profit organization to advance and connect women in technology, law and policy. Now international and boasting more than 2,000 members, ChIPs focuses on accelerating innovation through diversity of thought, participation and engagement to the benefit to society.

"Many people have been very supportive of me throughout my life and my career," Lee tells us. "I have a strong desire to give some of that back. Training and mentoring are important, because that's what opens the door for talented people to shine."

ELIZABETH ROSCOE is Vice President and Executive Director of the Western Union Foundation, a position she assumed in 2016, after having served in leadership positions not only for Western Union, but also for American Express, PepsiCo, Sainsbury's, Campbell's Soup, and Nestle. The Foundation has set a goal to provide 50,000 migrants, refugees, women and young adults with the skills they need to succeed in 21st century careers, by 2020. The goal is to focus on workforce training to maximize both the job opportunities available to them and their earning potential.

The Western Union Foundation is on track to meet its ambitious 2020 goal, and has been able to do this by leveraging Western Union employees, agents and consumers. "We asked Western Union employees—more than 12,000 in offices across the world—to nominate not-for-profit organizations in their communities that align with our mission to receive funding." She elaborates, "This global approach has allowed us to deepen our reach and work with not-for-profits so that they can grow and continue to connect disadvantaged young people to the global economy." Policy meets productivity in a world of inclusion.

ROSARIO LONDONO is a person who has lots of resume-worthy activities to her credit, but listing those, even with careful explanations, falls short of describing what she's about. Probably more than any other individual whom we have interviewed for this book, she is focused on the future and how you, we and everyone—yes, *every person in whatever country, position or what she might call "life space"*—should be able to help form that future. Yes, she's part of CNS Global Advisors, where she seeks to have an impact on investment and systems change. Yes, she's Co-founder of the DC-based League of Intrapreneurs. Yes, she offers a selection of online innovation tools, and actively searches for collaborators with whom she can improve the world we live in. So what she says is informed, impassioned, and proven by life and professional experience. She's not in the business of impressing people, though, so her thoughts are simple and forthright. And in a phrase, she captures the core of this book: "You constantly see views you usually don't see when all people come from the same background."

CLAUDIA MIRZA, the Founder and CEO of Akorbi, doesn't have just one story to tell, she has multiple life and business experiences that demonstrate how the melding of achievement and opportunity can produce almost unlimited success. Mirza's childhood in Colombia was marked by poverty and fear, enough so that it might have severed any hope of comfort, much less wealth. Yet the company she founded in 2003 is today a group of companies providing a variety of enterprise solutions, and the 13th fastest-growing woman-owned/led company in the world. As featured on its website, Akorbi's vision *(To be the sustainable partner for companies seeking to increase their global or diverse market position through innovation, language, and people.)* and values *(We are compassionate. We embrace excellence in all we do. We operate with integrity. We foster a fun, positive work environment. We are innovative.)* bespeak the results of Mirza's talent and drive, and as she tells us, the strength of the American dream:

> The United States is arguably the best environment for entrepreneurs to thrive. You need a support network. Our atmosphere here in America focuses on creating a space for business leaders: nonprofits, government agencies, and foundations. There is a support system provided by the universities and Small Business Administration to encourage women and immigrant leaders. Here in America people aren't afraid to share or to give advice. We are so diverse. Regardless of religion or economic class, we help. No one asks you what your faith is. People just want you to work. Regardless of your background. I've traveled to so many nations and have learned to value our American culture and our country.

ENDNOTES

1   https://www.theguardian.com/global/2018/nov/25/futurists-the-world-in-2050-science-medicine-food-travel-predictions.

2   https://www.brookings.edu/wp-content/uploads/2019/01/2019.01_BrookingsMetro_Automation-AI_Report_Muro-Maxim-Whiton-FINAL-version.pdf.

3   https://publicadmin.usc.edu/blog/the-relationship-between-corporations-and-public-policy-development/.

4   https://www.milkeninstitute.org/videos/view/the-business-case-for-equality-diversity-and-inclusion.

5   Carolyn Wiley and Mirela Monllor-Tormos, "Board Diversity in STEM&F Sectors: The Critical Mass Required to Drive Firm Performance," https://journals.sagepub.com/doi/abs/10.1177/1548051817750535.

6   https://www.forbes.com/sites/pamdanziger/2019/01/13/6-global-consumer-trends-and-brands-that-are-out-in-front-of-them-in-2019/#530c9d824fe4.

7   https://www.linkedin.com/pulse/every-once-while-new-technology-old-problem-big-idea-turn-fady-andary/.

8   https://www.strategy-business.com/article/Silicon-Valleys-Farsighted-Banker.

PERSPECTIVES ON POINT CONTRIBUTORS